AF609475

TELANGANA

A STATE STUDY GUIDE

NARAYAN REDDY

Published by

Hawk Press
4836/24, Ansari Road, Daryaganj
New Delhi – 110 002
Phones: 91-11-23278618, 91-11-43667199
E-mail: thehawkpress@gmail.com
www.thehawkpress.com

ISBN: 978-93-88318-90-7

Preface

Telangana is a state in the south of India. It is situated on the centre-south stretch of the Indian peninsula on the high Deccan Plateau. It is the twelfth largest state and the twelfth-most populated state in India with a geographical area of 112,077 km (43,273 sq mi) and 35,193,978 residents as per 2011 census. On 2 June 2014, the area was separated from the northwestern part of Andhra Pradesh as the newly formed 29th state with Hyderabad as its historic permanent capital. Its other major cities include Warangal, Nizamabad, Khammam and Karimnagar. Telangana is bordered by the states of Maharashtra to the north, Chhattisgarh to the east, Karnataka to the west and Andhra Pradesh to the east and south. The terrain of Telangana region consists mostly of hills, mountain ranges, and thick dense forests distribution of 27,292 sq. km. As of 2018, the state of Telangana is divided into 31 districts.

The cultural hearts of Telangana, Hyderabad and Warangal are noted for its wealth and renowned historical structures – Charminar, Qutb Shahi Tombs, Paigah Tombs, Falaknuma Palace, Chowmahalla Palace, Warangal Fort, Kakatiya Kala Thoranam, Thousand Pillar Temple and the Bhongir Fort in Yadadri Bhuvanagiri district. The historic city Golconda during the Kakatiya reign was once known for the mines that have produced some of the world's most famous gems, including the Koh-i-Noor, Hope Diamond, Daria-i-Noor, Regent Diamond, Nassak Diamond and Noor-ul-Ain. Religious edifices like the Lakshmi Narasimha Temple in Yadadri Bhuvanagiri district, Makkah Masjid in Hyderabad, and Medak Cathedral are several of its most famous places of worship.

Government of Telangana is a democratically elected body

that governs the State of Telangana, India. The state government is headed by the Governor of Telangana as the nominal head of state, with a democratically elected Chief Minister as the real head of the executive. The governor who is appointed for five years appoints the chief minister and his council of ministers. Even though the governor remains the ceremonial head of the state, the day-to-day running of the government is taken care of by the chief minister and his council of ministers in whom a great deal of legislative powers is vested. The state government maintains its capital at Hyderabad and is seated at the Government Secretariator the Sachivalayam.

The economy of Telangana is mainly supported by agriculture. Two important rivers of India, the Godavari and Krishna, flow through the state, providing irrigation. Farmers in Telangana mainly depend on rain-fed water sources for irrigation. Rice is the major food crop. Other important local crops are cotton, sugar cane, mango and tobacco. Recently, crops used for vegetable oil production, such as sunflower and peanuts, have gained favour. There are many multi-state irrigation projects in development, including Godavari River Basin Irrigation Projects.

The main players in the regional politics are the Telangana Rashtra Samithi, All India Majlis-e-Ittehadul Muslimeen, Telugu Desam Party, Bharatiya Janata Party and Indian National Congress. Following the Telangana Legislative Assembly Election in 2014, the Telangana Rashtra Samithi under Kalvakuntla Chandrashekar Rao was elected to power.

This is a reference book. All the matter is just compiled and edited in nature, taken from the various sources which are in public domain.

The book is intended to provide referral benefit to students, scholars and policy-makers.

—*Editor*

ABOUT THE BOOK

Telangana is a state in the south of India. It is situated on the centre-south stretch of the Indian peninsula on the high Deccan Plateau. It is the twelfth largest state and the twelfth-most populated state in India with a geographical area of 112,077 km (43,273 sq mi) and 35,193,978 residents as per 2011 census. On 2 June 2014, the area was separated from the northwestern part of Andhra Pradesh as the newly formed 29th state with Hyderabad as its historic permanent capital. Its other major cities include Warangal, Nizamabad, Khammam and Karimnagar. Telangana is bordered by the states of Maharashtra to the north, Chhattisgarh to the east, Karnataka to the west and Andhra Pradesh to the east and south. The terrain of Telangana region consists mostly of hills, mountain ranges, and thick dense forests distribution of 27,292 sq. km. As of 2018, the state of Telangana is divided into 31 districts. Government of Telangana is a democratically elected body that governs the State of Telangana, India. The state government is headed by the Governor of Telangana as the nominal head of state, with a democratically elected Chief Minister as the real head of the executive. The governor who is appointed for five years appoints the chief minister and his council of ministers. Telangana is governed by a parliamentary system of representative democracy, a feature the state shares with other Indian states. Universal suffrage is granted to residents. There are three branches of government. The book is intended to provide referral benefit to students, scholars and policy-makers.

Contents

1

State at a Glance

Telangana is a state in the south of India. It is situated on the centre-south stretch of the Indian peninsula on the high Deccan Plateau. It is the twelfth largest state and the twelfth-most populated state in India with a geographical area of 112,077 km (43,273 sq mi) and 35,193,978 residents as per 2011 census. On 2 June 2014, the area was separated from the northwestern part of Andhra Pradesh as the newly formed 29th state with Hyderabad as its historic permanent capital. Its other major cities include Warangal, Nizamabad, Khammam and Karimnagar. Telangana is bordered by the states of Maharashtra to the north, Chhattisgarh to the east, Karnataka to the west and Andhra Pradesh to the east and south. The terrain of Telangana region consists mostly of hills, mountain ranges, and thick dense forests distribution of 27,292 sq. km. As of 2018, the state of Telangana is divided into 31 districts.

Throughout antiquity and the Middle Ages, the region now known as Telangana was ruled by multiple major Indian powers such as the Mauryans, Satavahanas, Chalukyas, Kakatiyas, Delhi Sultanate, Bahmani Sultanate, Golconda Sultanate. During the 16th and 17th centuries, the region was ruled by the Mughals. The region is known for its *Ganga-Jamuni Tehzeeb*. During the 18th century and the British Raj, Telangana was ruled by the Nizam of Hyderabad. In 1823, the Nizams lost control over Northern Circars (Coastal Andhra) and Ceded

Districts (Rayalseema), which were handed over to the East India Company. The annexation by the British of the Northern Circars deprived Hyderabad State, the Nizam's dominion, of the considerable coastline it formerly had, to that of a landlocked princely state with territories in Central Deccan, bounded on all sides by British India. Thereafter, the Northern Circars were governed as part of Madras Presidency until India's independence in 1947, after which the presidency became India's Madras state.

The Hyderabad state joined the Union of India in 1948 after an Indian military invasion. In 1956, the Hyderabad State was dissolved as part of the linguistic reorganisation of states and Telangana was merged with the Telugu-speaking Andhra State (part of the Madras Presidency during the British Raj) to form Andhra Pradesh. A peasant-driven movement began to advocate for separation from Andhra Pradesh starting in the early 1950s, and continued until Telangana was awarded separate statehood on 2 June 2014.

The economy of Telangana is the eighth-largest state economy in India with 8.43 lakh crore (US$120 billion) in gross domestic product and a per capita GDP of 181,000 (US$2,500). The state has emerged as a major focus for robust IT software, Industryand Services sector. The state is also the main administrative centre to a large number of Indian defence aero-space and research labs like Bharat Dynamics Limited, Defence Metallurgical Research Laboratory, Defence Research and Development Organisationand Defence Research and Development Laboratory.

The cultural hearts of Telangana, Hyderabad and Warangal are noted for its wealth and renowned historical structures – Charminar, Qutb Shahi Tombs, Paigah Tombs, Falaknuma Palace, Chowmahalla Palace, Warangal Fort, Kakatiya Kala Thoranam, Thousand Pillar Temple and the Bhongir Fort in Yadadri Bhuvanagiri district. The historic city Golconda during the Kakatiya reign was once known for the mines that have produced some of the world's most famous gems, including the Koh-i-Noor, Hope Diamond, Daria-i-Noor, Regent Diamond,

Nassak Diamond and Noor-ul-Ain. Religious edifices like the Lakshmi Narasimha Temple in Yadadri Bhuvanagiri district, Makkah Masjid in Hyderabad, and Medak Cathedral are several of its most famous places of worship.

ETYMOLOGY

A popular etymology derives the word "Telangana" from *Trilinga desa* ("land of three lingas"), a region so called because three important Shaivite shrines were located here: Kaleshwaram, Srisailam and Draksharama. According to Jayadhir Thirumala Rao, a former director of Andhra Pradesh Oriental Manuscripts Library and Research Centre, the name Telangana is of Gondi origin. Rao asserts that it is derived from "Telangadh", which according to him, means "south" in Gondi and has been referred to in "Gond script dating back to about 2000 years".

One of the earliest uses of a word similar to Telangana can also be seen in a name of Malik Maqbul (14th century CE), who was called the *Tilangani*, which implies that he was from Tilangana. He was the commander of the Warangal Fort (*Kataka Pâludu*).

A 16th Century travel writer Ferishta recorded in his book:

During the just reign of Ibrahim Kootb Shah, *Tulingana* like Egypt, became the mart of the whole world. Merchants from Toorkistan, Arabia and Persia, resorted to it ; and they met with such encouragement that they found in it inducements to return frequently. The greatest luxuries from foreign parts daily abounded at the king's hospitable board.

The word "Telinga" changed over time to "Telangana" and the name "Telangana" was designated to distinguish the predominantly Telugu-speaking region of the erstwhile Hyderabad State from its predominantly Marathi-speaking one, Marathwada. After Asaf Jahis ceded the Seemandhra region to the British, the rest of the Telugu region retained the name Telingana and the other parts were called Madras Presidency's Circars and Ceded.

CURRENT SCENARIO OF TELANGANA

While the jury is still out on the need for bifurcation of Andhra Pradesh into Telangana and Andhra State on June 4, 2014 in the first instance, the former with just 10 districts and being landlocked will have to depend to a large extend on the latter for boosting trade and commerce.

Yes, of course Hyderabad will be the capital of Telangana which will reap dividend on the enormous investment pouring into the twin city (including Secunderabad) in software and other sectors.

But the question that begs a ready answer is: Will Telangana, the 29th state of Indian Union, be able to compete with others in terms of industrialisation, economic growth and social progress in health and education given its geographical positioning and the dearth of resources that will be felt unlike Andhra which has the longest eastern coastline, besides a thriving agriculture and village-based industries.

According to Telangana Rashtra Samiti (TRS) chief and Telangana chief minister K. Chandrashekar Rao this region has been long neglected whereas Seemandhra regions made steady progress since 1956 after Hyderabad State merged with Telugu-speaking areas of Madras Presidency.

Further, he claims that except for capital Hyderabad which was the real beneficiary of the software bóom and rode high on the spate of investments for new projects, the rest of Telangana were mired deep in poverty and social negligence.

Same culture, language, but yet divided

It may look strange to an outsider, but it looks Telangana would have done better if it had been part of united Andhra rather than creating its own statehood in the name of justice for its people and region which was allegedly neglected for long.

While Andhra consisting of coastal Andhra and Rayalaseema (jointly called Seemandhra) has plenty of mineral resources and fertile soil with Krishna and Godavari rivers irrigating the fields, Telangana has nothing to boast of except for its showcase

IT city Hyderabad, the capital of Nizam's kingdom of a bygone era.

According to spiritual guru Sri Sri Ravi Shankar, "Over a third of the economy of the entire state (united Andhra) is based in the capital (Hyderabad). This being the condition, it is the coastal Andhra or Rayal Seema people who should have demanded a separate state for self governance. While these two regions do not want to separate, there is no logic for people in the capital not wanting to have their association with Andhra."

Further, Ravi Shankar feels that it "appears completely unfair to push away people when they want to be a part of united Andhra Pradesh. If the Nizam was alive, he would have loved to have more area in his state rather than shrink it."

Will business move out of Hyderabad?

There is a genuine fear that once Telangana was formed, businesses would shift their bases to Seemandhra. The port city of Visakhapatnam is being developed into an industrial hub with a number of units in pharma and software, apart from being the naval headquarters for the Eastern Command.

Seemandhra people run most of the factories, offices and plants in Hyderabad and they may return to their own places and create a number of industrial hubs.

The fear of Naxalites taking control of large parts of Telangana may hit business hard in Hyderabad even as Andhra can develop major cities like Visakhapatnam, Vijayawada, Rajahmundry, Tirupati, Ongole and Kurnool.

Importance of Hyderabad to Telangana

This high-tech metro contributes 55% of state's (united Andhra) total revenue of Rs 70,000 crore. The city is a major software hub in India with 1,300 MNCs and offers employment to 5 lakh highly skilled workforce in this sector.

While accounting for over 90% of the state's IT exports worth Rs 40,000 crore, Hyderabad ranks fourth in terms of software exports from India.

KCR faces daunting challenges

Having achieved Telangana statehood, TRS chief and Chief Minister K. Chandrasekhar Rao has his work cut out - to frame policies for even growth of industries across the 10 districts of the state where social and economic backwardness have pushed the people into the clutches of naxalites.

At the same time, he should avoid the present bickerings with Andhra's ruling TDP and its CM Chandrababu Naidu for a number of real and petty issues and instead extend the hand of cooperative friendship for a win-win situation of both Telangana and Andhra. So, that these two states divided by common culture and language due to the alleged regional disparities can march forward in a friendly competitive spirit.

HISTORY OF TELANGANA

The history of Telangana, located in the Deccan region, includes its governance by many rulers. It was ruled by the Satavahana dynasty (230 BCE to 220 CE), the Telinga Kakatiya Dynasty (1083–1323), the Musunuri Nayaks (1326–1356) the Delhi Sultanate, the Bahmani Sultanate (1347–1509) and Vijayanagara Empire (1509–1529). Later, the Telangana region became part of the Golconda Sultanate (1529–1687) and Hyderabad State (1724-1948).

On 2 June 2014, Telangana became the 29th state of India, consisting of the thirty-one districts, with Hyderabad as its capital. The city of Hyderabad will continue to serve as the joint capital for Andhra Pradesh and the successor state of Telangana for a period of ten years.

The histories of Telangana and of Andhra Pradesh are very similar as both states share the same language and culture.

Telangana was governed by many rulers, including the Maurya Empire(320 BCE to 180 BCE), Satavahana dynasty (180 BCE to 220 CE), Vakataka dynasty (250CE - 500CE), Chalukya dynasty (543CE - 753CE), Rashtrakuta dynasty (753CE - 982CE), the Kakatiya Dynasty (1083CE –1323CE), the Musunuri Nayaks (1326–1356) the Delhi Sultanate, the

Bahmani Sultanate (1347–1512), Vijayanagara Empire (1336–1646), Qutb Shahi dynasty (1512–1687), Mughal Empire (1687–1724) and Asaf Jahi Dynasty (1724–1948).

Early history

The Satavahana dynasty (230 BCE to 220 CE) became the dominant power in this region. It originated from the lands between the Godavari and Krishna rivers and was based at Amaravathi and Dharanikota.

After the decline of the Satavahanas, various dynasties, such as the Vakataka, Vishnukundina, Chalukya, Rashtrakuta and Western Chalukya, ruled the area.

Kakatiya Dynasty

Ramagiri Fort ruins at Kalvacherlain Karimnagar district is an ancient fort initially built by the Sathavahanas and modified many times by other dynasties till 16th century.

The Telangana area experienced its golden age during the reign of the Kakatiya dynasty, which ruled most parts of the present-day Andhra Pradesh and Telangana from 1083 to 1323 CE. Rudrama Devi and Prataparudra II were prominent rulers from the Kakatiya dynasty. The dynasty weakened with the attack of Malik Kafur in 1309 and was dissolved after the defeat of Prataparudra by the forces of Muhammad bin Tughluq in 1323.

Kota Gullu, temple ruins built in the 12th century by Kakatiyas at Ghanpur, Mulug in Warangal district.

Qutb Shahi and Asaf Jahi's

Golkonda Fort

The area came under the rule of the Delhi Sultanate in the 14th century, followed by the Bahmani Sultanate. Quli Qutb Mulk, a governor of Golkonda, revolted against the Bahmani

Sultanate and established the Qutb Shahi dynasty in 1518. On 21 September 1687, the Golkonda Sultanate came under the rule of the Mughal emperor Aurangzeb after a year-long siege of the Golkonda fort.

Telangana was the seat of numerous dynasties. The Chowmahalla Palace was home to the Nizams of Hyderabad.

In 1712, Qamar-ud-din Khan was appointed by emperor Farrukhsiyar as the viceroy of Deccan with the title *Nizam-ul-Mulk* (meaning "Administrator of the Realm"). He was later recalled to Delhi, with Mubariz Khan appointed as the viceroy. In 1724, Qamar-ud-din Khan defeated Mubariz Khan to reclaim the *Deccan suba,* establishing it as an autonomous province of the Mughal empire.

He took the name *Asif Jah*, starting what came to be known as the Asif Jahi dynasty. He named the area Hyderabad Deccan. Subsequent rulers retained the title *Nizam ul-Mulk* and were called Asif Jahi Nizams or nizams of Hyderabad. The Medak and Warangal divisions of Telangana were part of their realm.

When Asif Jah I died in 1748, there was political unrest due to contention for the throne among his sons, who were aided by opportunistic neighbouring states and colonial foreign forces. In 1769, Hyderabad city became the formal capital of the Nizams. The Nizam Nasir-ud-dawlah, Asaf Jah IV signed the Subsidiary Alliance with the British in 1799 and lost its control over the state's defence and foreign affairs. Hyderabad State became a princely state among the presidencies and provinces of British India.

Post-independence

When India became independent from the British Empire in 1947, the Nizam of Hyderabad did not want to merge with the Indian Union and wanted to remain independent. The Government of India annexed Hyderabad State on 17 September 1948 after a military operation called Operation Polo. It appointed a civil servant, M. K. Vellodi, as first chief minister of Hyderabad State on 26 January 1950. He administered the state with the help of English-educated bureaucrats from the Madras and Bombay states, who were familiar with British systems of administration unlike the bureaucrats of Hyderabad State who used a completely different administrative system. The official language of the state was switched from Urdu to English.

In 1952, Dr. Burgula Ramakrishna Rao was elected chief minister of the Hyderabad State in its first democratic election. During this time, there were violent agitations by some

Telanganites to send the Madras state bureaucrats back and implement a rule by the natives (*mulkis*) of Hyderabad (Syed alam sharjil) was elected chief minister of Hyderabad after (Dr Burgula Ramakrishana Rao) for one year he has given resign from the post.

Telangana Rebellion

The Telangana Rebellion was a peasant revolt supported by the communists. It originated in the Telangana regions of the Hyderabad Statebetween 1946 and 1951, led by the Communist Party of India (CPI).

The revolt began in the Nalgonda district against the feudal lords of Reddy and Velama castes. It quickly spread to the Warangal and Bidardistricts.

Peasant farmers and labourers revolted against the local feudal landlords (*jagirdars* and *deshmukhs*) and later against the Nizam Osman Ali Khan. The violent phase of the movement ended after the Government of India's Operation Polo. Starting in 1951, the CPI shifted to a more moderate strategy of seeking to bring communism to India within the framework of Indian democracy.

States Reorganisation Commission

In December 1953, the States Reorganisation Commission (SRC) was appointed to form states on a linguistic basis. An agreement was reached between Telangana leaders and Andhra leaders on 20 February 1956 to merge Telangana and Andhra with promises to safeguard Telangana's interests. After reorganisation in 1956, the region of Telangana was merged with Andhra State to form Andhra Pradesh.

Following this Gentlemen's agreement, the central government established the unified state of Andhra Pradesh on 1 November 1956. G.O 553 of 1959 from the united Andhra Pradesh state moved two revenue divisions of Bhadrachalam from East Godavariand Aswaraopeta from West Godavari to Khammam for administrative convenience.

Telangana movement

There have been several movements to revoke the merger of Telangana and Andhra, major ones occurring in 1969, 1972 and 2009. The movement for a new state of Telangana gained momentum in the 21st century by an initiative of Telangana Political Joint Action Committee, TJAC including political leadership representing Telangana area. On 9 December 2009 the Government of India announced the process of formation of the Telangana state. Violent protests led by people in the Coastal Andhra and Rayalseema regions occurred immediately after the announcement, and the decision was put on hold on 23 December 2009.

The movement continued in Hyderabad and other districts of Telangana. There have been hundreds of claimed suicides, strikes, protests and disturbances to public life demanding separate statehood.

Formation of Telangana state in 2014

On 30 July 2013, the Congress Working Committee unanimously passed a resolution to recommend the formation of a separate Telangana state. After various stages the bill was placed in the Parliament of India in February 2014. In February 2014, Andhra Pradesh Reorganisation Act, 2014 bill was passed by the Parliament of India for the formation of Telangana state comprising ten districts from north-western Andhra Pradesh. The bill received the assent of the President and published in the Gazette on 1 March 2014.

The state of Telangana was officially formed on 2 June 2014. Kalvakuntla Chandrashekar Rao was elected as the first chief minister of Telangana, following elections in which the Telangana Rashtra Samithi party secured majority. Hyderabad will remain as the joint capital of both Telangana and Andhra Pradesh for a period, not more than 10 years after that period Hyderabad shall be the capital of the State of Telangana and there shall be a new capital for the State of Andhra Pradesh.

Andhra Pradesh picked Amaravati as its capital and moved its secretariat in 2016 and legislature in March 2017 to its new capital.

EARLY HISTORY

Satavahana Dynasty

The Satavahanas rose to a political power, after the fall of the Mauryan Empire. Koti Lingala seems to be one of the 30 cities of Satavahana dynasty. Excavations revealed brick wells, coins belonging to a pre-Satavahana period, namely, Gobhada and Samagopa.

It is believed that the place is the site of the hermitage of sage Bhavari. Several coins of Simukha, the founder of the Satavahana dynasty, and those of other early rulers like Kanha and Satakarni I were found.

The Deccan, during this period, was an emporium of inland and maritime trade. The region between the rivers of Godavari and Krishna was full of ports and throbbing with activity. There was plentiful of currency to facilitate trade and the people entered upon a period of great industrial, commercial and maritime activity.

Buddhism flourished throughout the period and the rulers were also devoted to Vedic ritualism. They constructed several Buddhist Stupas, Viharas and Chaityas. Satavahanas were able rulers and loved literacy and architecture.

The 17th ruler of this dynasty, Hâla was a great poet and his "Gathasaptasati" in Prakrit was well received by all. Gunadhya, the minister of Hala was the author of "Brihatkadha". According to Matsya Purana, there were 29 rulers of this dynasty. They ruled over for about 456 years, from the 2nd century BC to the 2nd century AD. The empire included most of the southern peninsula and some southern parts of the present Indian states of Maharashtra, Orissa and Madhya Pradesh. The court language used by the Satavahanas was Prakrit.

The decline and fall of the Satavahana Empire left the state in a political chaos. Local rulers, as well as invaders, tried to carve out small kingdoms for themselves and to establish many dynasties. Such instability continued to prevail until the rise of the Western Chalukyas.

Kakatiya dynasty

Kakatiya Kala Thoranam at Warangal Fort

The 12th and 13th centuries saw the emergence of the Kakatiya dynasty. The Kakatiyas are known for their famous architecture such as Warangal Fort, Ramappa Temple,

Thousand Pillar Temple and Kota Gullu. At first they were feudatories of the Western Chalukyas of Kalyani, ruling over a small territory near Warangal.

A ruler of this dynasty, Prola II (1110–1158), extended his sway to the south and declared his independence. His successor Rudra (1158–1195) pushed the kingdom to the east up to the Godavari delta.

He built Warangal Fort to serve as a second capital and faced the invasions of the Seuna Yadavas of Devagiri. The next ruler, Mahadeva, extended the kingdom to the coastal area. Ganapati Deva succeeded him in 1199. He was the greatest of the Kakatiyas and the first after the Satavahanas to bring almost the entire Telugu area under one unified empire. Ganapati put an end to the rule of the Velanati Cholas in 1210 and extended his empire to Anakapalle in the north.

The most prominent ruler in this dynasty was Rani Rudrama Devi (1262–1289), one of the few queens in Indian history. An able fighter and ruler, Rudrama defended the kingdom against the Cholas and the Seuna Yadavas, earning their respect. Marco Polo visited India during her reign and made note of her rule in flattering terms.

On the death of Rudrama at the beginning of 1290, her grandson Prataparudra II ascended the throne. Prataparudra had to fight battles throughout his reign against either internal rebels or external foes. Prataparudra expanded his borders to the west to Raichur and in the south to Ongole and the Nallamala Hills, whilst introducing many administrative reforms, some of which were also later adopted in the Vijayanagar empire.

In 1309, the Sultan of Delhi, Alauddin Khilji sent his general Malik Kafur on an expedition to the Kakatiyakingdom. Kafur's army reached the Kakatiya capital Warangal in January 1310, and breached its outer fort after a month-long siege. The Kakatiya ruler Prataparudra decided to surrender and agreed to pay tribute. Kafur returned to Delhi in June 1310 with a huge amount of wealth obtained from the defeated king. The Koh-i-Noordiamond was said to be among the loot.

Invasion by Delhi Sultanate

In 1323, Ghiyath al-Din Tughluq sent his son Ulugh Khan on an expedition to the Kakatiya capital of Warangal. The ensuing Siege of Warangal resulted in the annexation of Warangal, and the end of the Kakatiya dynasty.Prataparudra was taken captive, and sent to Delhi, but it is believed he died en route. Ulugh Khan ruled briefly as viceroy, until he returned to Delhi to succeed the throne.

As early as 1330, the Musunuri Nayaks who served as army chiefs for Kakatiya kingdom united the various Telugu clans and recovered Warangal from the viceroy of the Delhi Sultanate and ruled for half a century. Surrounded by more significant states, by the 15th century these new entities had ceded to the Bahmani Sultanate and the Sangama dynasty, the latter of which evolved to become the Vijayanagara empire.

BAHMANI AND DECCAN SULTANATES

The Qutb Shahi Monuments of Hyderabad were submitted by India in the tentative list for UNESCO World Heritage status in 2011.

Charminar

One of the Qutb Shahi tombs

Golconda Fort

The Bahmani Sultanate ruled the region in the 15th century. In 1463, Sultan Muhammad Shah Bahmani II dispatched Sultan Quli Qutb-ul-Mulk to the Telangana region to quell disturbances. Sultan Quli quelled the disturbance and was rewarded as the administrator of the region. He established a base at Kakatiya hill fortress of Golconda which he strengthened and expanded considerably. By the end of the century, Quli ruled from Golconda as the *subedar* (governor) of the Telangana region. Quli enjoyed virtual independence from Bidar, where the Bahmani Sultanate was then based. In 1518, when the Bahmani Sultanate disintegrated into five different kingdoms, with the others based in Ahmednagar, Berar, Bidar and Bijapur. Sultan Quli declared independence from the Bahmani rule and established the Golconda Sultanate under the title "Sultan Quli Qutub Shah", he rebuilt the mud-fort of Golconda and named the city *Muhammad Nagar*.

During this period, the city of Hyderabad was established by Muhammad Quli Qutb Shah in 1591, on the banks of the Musi River. The Charminar and Mecca Masjid were constructed to form a centerpiece of the city. Over the years, Hyderabad would grow as an important trading center for diamonds, pearls, arms and steel.

The Qutb Shahi rulers were patrons of both Indo-Persian and the local Telugu art and culture. Early Indo-Islamictype of architecture is reflected in the Qutb Shahi buildings. Some examples of it include the Golconda Fort, Qutb Shahi tombs, Char Minar, Mecca Masjid, Khairtabad Mosque, Taramati Baradari and Toli Mosque.

MUGHAL CONQUEST AND RULE

Mughal prince Aurangzeb spent most of his time in the Deccan, fighting local Hindu and Muslim kingdoms alike to establish Mughal sovereignty. The Golconda Sultanate faced various attacks by the Mughal prince Aurangzeb, who was appointed Viceroy of the Deccan by his father and Mughal Emperor Shah Jahan. It was forced to pay an annual tribute to the Mughal Empire.

In 1656, Aurangzeb attacked Golconda Fort by surprise but was forced to call of the siege on orders of Shah Jahan. Therefore, a treaty was signed between Abdullah Qutb Shah and Aurangzeb, when the former accepted Mughal sovereignty, paid an annual tribute and married his daughter to Aurangzeb's eldest son.

After becoming Mughal Emperor, Aurangzeb returned to the Deccan. He captured Hyderabad and besieged Golconda in 1687, and the refused any negotiations. On September 22, 1687, after a nine month long siege, Golconda was captured. Abul Hasan Qutb Shah was taken prisoner, and Hyderabad's diamond trade was all but destroyed.

NIZAMS OF HYDERABAD

The Nizams of Hyderabad, also known as the *Asaf Jahi* dynasty, ruled Hyderabad State, which comprised Telangana, Marathwada and Hyderabad-Karnataka from 1724 to 1948. Under this period, Hyderabad State was the largest princely statein British India, and had its own mint, currency, railway and postal system. The Nizam acquired massive amounts of wealth due to the diamond trade.

Asaf Jah I

With the emaciation of the Mughal Empire after Aurangzeb's death in 1707, the Mughal-appointed governors of the *Deccan Suba* (Deccan province) gained more autonomy from Delhi. In 1714, the Mughal Emperor Farrukhsiyar appointed Mir Qamar-ud-din Siddiqi as the viceroy to the Deccan and gave him the title of *Nizam-ul-Mulk (governor of the country)*. He was well suited for the position as he had fought alongside his father and grandfather who were commanders during the siege of Golconda.

In 1724, he defeated Mubariz Khan to establish control over Hyderabad. He received the title of *Asaf Jah* from Mughal Emperor Muhammad Shah in the following year. Thus began the Asaf Jahi dynasty that would rule Hyderabad State until a year after India's independence from Britain.

Successors of Asaf Jah I

When Asaf Jah I died in 1748, there was political unrest due to contention for the throne among his sons, who were aided by opportunistic neighbouring states and colonial foreign forces.

The death of Asaf Jah I in 1748 resulted in a period of political unrest as his sons, backed by opportunistic neighbouring states and colonial foreign forces, contended for the throne. The accession of Asif Jah II, who reigned from 1762 to 1803, ended the instability. In 1768 he signed the Treaty of Machilipatnam, surrendering the coastal region to the East India Company in return for a fixed annual rent.

In 1769 Hyderabad city became the formal capital of the Nizams. In response to regular threats from Hyder Ali (*Dalwai* of Mysore), Baji Rao I (*Peshwa* of the Maratha Empire), and Basalath Jung (Asaf Jah II's elder brother, who was supported by the Marquis de Bussy-Castelnau), the Nizam signed a subsidiary alliance with the East India Company in 1798, allowing the British Indian Army to occupy Bolarum (modern Secunderabad) to protect the state's capital, for which the Nizams paid an annual maintenance to the British.

When the British and the French spread their hold over the country, successive Nizams won their friendship without bequeathing their power. The Nizams allied themselves with each side at different times, playing a significant role in the Anglo-Mysore Wars.

The Great Musi flood of 1908 ravaged the city of Hyderabad and resulted in the death of at least 15,000 people.

In 1911, Mir Osman Ali Khan, the seventh and last Nizam of Hyderabad succeeded his father. He was widely known for his wealth and considered one of the wealthiest men of all time. The development of early modern Hyderabad took place during his reign.

Telangana Rebellion

In late 1945, there started a peasant uprising in Telangana area, led by the Comrades Association (representing Communist Party of India) also known as The Telangana Rebellion or *Vetti Chakiri Udyamam* or *Telangana Raithanga Sayudha Poratam*. The communists drew their support from various quarters.

Among the poor peasants, there were grievances against the *jagirdari* system, which covered 43% of landholding. Initially, they also drew support from wealthier peasants who also fought under the communist banner, but by 1948, the coalition had disintegrated. According to the Indian intelligence Bureau Deputy Director, the social and economic programs of the communists were "positive and in some cases great... The communists redistributed land and livestock, reduced rates, ended forced labor and increased wages by one hundred percent. They inoculated the population and built public latrines; they encouraged women's organisations, discouraged sectarian sentiment and sought to abolish untouchability."

Initially, in 1945, the communists targeted *zamindars* and *deshmukhs*, but soon they launched a full-fledged revolt against the Nizam. Starting mid-1946, the conflict between the *Razakars* (a private militia led by Kasim Razvi) and the communists became increasingly violent, with both sides resorting to increasingly brutal methods. The *Razakars*cordoned off villages, captured suspected communists en masse and engaged in 'absolutely indiscriminate and organised' (according to one Congressman) looting and massacres. According to an Indian government pamphlet, the communists had killed about 2,000 people by 1948.

POST-INDEPENDENCE

India became independent from the United Kingdom in 1947. The Nizam of Hyderabad wanted to retain his independence from India, but was forced to cede his state to India in 1948 to form Hyderabad State.

Indian integration of Hyderabad

Operation Polo, the code name of the Hyderabad "Police Action" was a military operation in September 1948 in which the Indian Armed Forces invaded the State of Hyderabad and overthrew its Nizam, annexing the state into the Indian Union.

At the time of the Partition of India, the princely states of India, who in principle had self-government within their own territories, were subject to subsidiary alliances with the British, giving them control of their external relations. In the Indian Independence Act 1947 the British abandoned all such alliances, leaving the states with the option of opting for full independence. However, by 1948 almost all had acceded to either India or Pakistan.

One major exception was that of Hyderabad, where the Nizam, a Muslim ruler who presided over a largely Hindu population, chose independence and hoped to maintain this with an irregular army recruited from the Muslim aristocracy, known as the *Razakars*. The Nizam was also beset by the Telangana uprising, which he was unable to subjugate.

The Indian government, anxious to avoid what it termed a Balkanization of what had been the Indian Empire, was determined on the integration of Hyderabad State into the new Indian Union. Amidst atrocities by the *Razakars*, the Indian Home Minister Sardar Patel decided to annex Hyderabad in what was termed a "police action". The operation itself took five days, in which the Razakars were defeated easily.

The operation led to massive violence on communal lines. The Indian prime minister Jawaharlal Nehru appointed a commission known as the Sunderlal Committee. Its report, which was not released until 2013, concluded that "as a conservative estimate, 27,000 to 40,000 people had lost their lives during and after the police action."

Hyderabad State (1948–1956)

After Operation Polo, the Hyderabad State was formed and Mir Osman Ali Khan served as Rajapramukh. M. K. Vellodi was elected Chief Minister of Hyderabad State.

Andhra Pradesh (1956–2014)

In December 1953, the States Reorganisation Commission (SRC) was appointed to form states on a linguistic basis. An agreement was reached between Telangana leaders and Andhra leaders on 20 February 1956 to merge Telangana and Andhra with promises to safeguard Telangana's interests. After reorganization in 1956, the region of Telangana was merged with Andhra State to form Andhra Pradesh.

Telangana State (2014–present)

On 30 July 2013, the Congress Working Committee unanimously passed a resolution to recommend the formation of a separate Telangana state. After various stages the bill was placed in the Parliament of India in February 2014. In February 2014, Andhra Pradesh Reorganisation Act, 2014 bill was passed by the Parliament of India for the formation of Telangana state comprising ten districts from north-western Andhra Pradesh. The bill received the assent of the President on 1 March 2014.

The state of Telangana was officially formed on 2 June 2014. Kalvakuntla Chandrashekar Rao was elected as the first chief minister of Telangana, following elections in which the Telangana Rashtra Samithi party secured majority. Hyderabad will remain as the joint capital of both Telangana and Andhra Pradesh for a period, not more than 10 years.

TELANGANA REBELLION

The Telangana Rebellion was a peasant rebellion against the feudal lords of the Telangana region and, later, the princely state of Hyderabad, between 1946 and 1951.

Communist involvement

The communists were as surprised as everyone else to see their efforts culminate in a series of successful attempts at organising the rebellion and distribution of land. With the Nizam holding on, even after the proclamation of Indian independence, the communists stepped up their campaign, stating that the flag of the Indian union was also the flag of the people of Hyderabad, much against the wishes of the ruling Asaf Jah dynasty.

Events

The revolt started in 1946 against the oppressive feudal lords and quickly spread to the Warangal and Bidar districts in around 4000 villages. Peasant farmers and labourers revolted against local feudal landlords (*jagirdars* and *deshmukhs*), who were ruling the villages known as samsthans. These samsthans were ruled mostly by Deshasthas, Reddys and Velama, known as *doralu*.

They ruled over the communities in the village and managed the tax collections (revenues) and owned almost all the land in that area. The Nizam had little control over these regions except the capital, Hyderabad. Chakali Ilamma, belonging to the Rajaka caste, had revolted against 'zamindar' Ramachandra Reddy, during the struggle when he tried to take her 4 acres of land. Her revolt inspired many to join the movement.

The agitation led by communists was successful in taking over 3000 villages from the feudal lords and 10,00,000 acres of agriculture land was distributed to landless peasants. Around 4000 peasants lost their lives in the struggle fighting feudal private armies.

It later became a fight against Nizam Osman Ali Khan, Asif Jah VII. The initial modest aims were to do away with the illegal and excessive exploitation meted out by these feudal lords in the name of bonded labour. The most strident demand was for the writing off of all debts of the peasants that were manipulated by the feudal lords.

NIZAM'S RESISTANCE TO JOIN INDIA

With Hyderabad's administration failing after 1945, the Nizam succumbed to the pressure of the Muslim elite and started the Razzakar Movement. At the same, time the Nizam was resisting the Indian government's efforts to bring the Hyderabad state into the Indian Union. The government sent the army in September 1948 to annex the Hyderabad state into Indian Union. The Communist party had already instigated the peasants to use guerrilla tactics against the Razzakars and around 3000 villages (about 41000 km) had come under peasant rule. The landlords were either killed or driven out and the land was redistributed. These victorious villages established communes reminiscent of Soviet mirs to administer their region.

These community governments were integrated regionally into a central organization. The rebellion was led by the Communist Party of India under the banner of Andhra Mahasabha.

Among the well-known individuals at the forefront of the movement were Ravi Narayana Reddy, Maddikayala Omkar, Maddikayala Lakshmi Omkar, Puchalapalli Sundarayya, Pillaipalli Papireddy, Suddala Hanmanthu, Chandra Rajeswara Rao, Bommagani Dharma Bhiksham, Makhdoom Mohiuddin, Sulaiman Areeb, Hassan Nasir, Manthrala Adi Reddy, Bhimreddy Narasimha Reddy,Nandyala Srinivas Reddy, Mallu Venkata Narasimha Reddy, Mallu Swarajyam, Lankala Raghava Reddy, Kukudal Jangareddy, Aruthla Ramchandra Reddy, Krishna Murthy, Aruthula Kamaladevi and Bikumalla Sathyam.

The violent phase of the movement ended in 1951, when the last guerilla squads were subdued in the Telangana region.

Annexation of Hyderabad State

The rebellion and the subsequent police action led to the capture of Hyderabad state from the Nizam's rule on 17 September 1948 and after a temporary military administration the dominion was eventually merged into the Indian Union. In the process tens of thousands of people lost their lives, the majority that died during the army's movement were Muslims. According to Sunderlal report which hasn't been officially released estimates that around 50,000 Muslims were massacred. Other estimates by responsible observers run as high as 200,000.. The Communist Party of India, although weak today, still retains strong support in the grassroots of Telangana. Puchchalapalli Sundaraiah went on to become the first leader of opposition in independent India.

The last Nizam Asaf Jah VII was made the Rajpramukh of the Hyderabad State from 26 January 1950 to 31 October 1956. The 1952 elections led to the victory of the Congress party in Hyderabad state. Burgula Ramakrishna Rao was first Chief Minister of the Hyderabad state from 1952 to 1956. In 1956, Hyderabad State was merged with Andhra State to form

Andhra Pradesh. It was again separated from Andhra Pradesh to establish the State of Telangana in 2014.

Land reform

The revolt ensured the victory of the Communist Party in Andhra Pradesh in the 1952 elections. Land reforms were recognised as important and various acts were passed to implement them.

SPORTS

Rajiv Gandhi International Cricket Stadium

The Hyderabad cricket team is represented in the Ranji Trophy and has won twice. The SunRisers Hyderabad, an Indian Premier Leaguefranchise, is based in Hyderabad and has won the trophy once.

Deccan Chargers, a currently defunct franchise from Hyderabad, also won the Indian Premier League once. The Rajiv Gandhi International Cricket Stadium is the home ground of both Hyderabad cricket team and SunRisers Hyderabad. It hosts international as well as domestic matches. The Hyderabad Hunters, a Premier Badminton League franchise, the Telugu Titans, a Pro Kabaddi League franchise, the Hyderabad Sky, a UBA Pro Basketball League franchise, the Telugu Tigers, a Premier Futsal franchise are also based in Hyderabad. Hyderabad Hunters won the Premier Badminton League title once.

Notable sports persons from the state are Mohammad Azharuddin, V. V. S. Laxman, Mithali Raj, Pragyan Ojha, Saina Nehwal, P.V. Sindhu, Jwala Gutta, Parupalli Kashyap, Gagan Narang, Mukesh Kumar and Pullela Gopichand (Andhra Pradesh), as well as Sania Mirza who has been appointed as the "brand ambassador" of Telangana.

Other stadiums include G. M. C. Balayogi Athletic Stadium, Lal Bahadur Shastri Stadium and Gachibowli Indoor Stadium.

2

Culture and Society

CULTURE OF TELANGANA

The Indian state of Telangana has a cultural history of about 5,000 years. The region emerged as the foremost centre of culture in Indian subcontinent during the rule of Hindu Kakatiya dynasty and the Muslim Qutb Shahi and Asaf Jahi dynasties— (also known as the Nizams of Hyderabad). The rulers' patronage and interest for arts and culture transformed Telangana into a unique multi-cultural region where two different cultures coexist together, thus making Telangana the representative of the Deccan Plateau and its heritage with Warangal and Hyderabad being its epicenter. The regions' major cultural events celebrated are "Kakatiya Festival" and Deccan Festival along with religious festivals Bonalu, Bathukamma, Dussehra, Ugadi, Sankranthi, Milad un Nabi and Ramadan.

Telangana State has long been a meeting place for diverse languages and cultures. It is known as "South of North and North of South". It is also known for its Ganga-Jamuna Tehzeeb and the capital Hyderabad is known as a *miniature India.*

Telangana Culture

In Deccan region one can witness the vibrant blend of Telugu culture existing from the times of Satavahanas (230

BCE - 220 CE) and Kakatiyas (1175-1324 CE) and Persian traditions from the Mughals and Nizams (1724-1948)who ruled before and during the reign of British imperialism respectively.

While Telugu is the predominant language with 76% of the people speaking it, Urdu (12%) and other languages (12%) are also quite common in this region Before 1948, Urdu was the official language of the princely state of Hyderabad and it was the common dialect among the elite of Telangana.

However, Telugu became the official language and was introduced as the medium of instruction in schools and colleges after Hyderabad joined the Indian Union, following which the use of Urdu among non-Muslim was reduced.

Kakatiya Kala Thoranam

Telangana culture combines cultural customs from Persian traditions, embedded during the rule of the region by the Moghuls, Qutub Shahis and Nizams, with prominent and predominantly south Indian traditions and customs. The State has a rich tradition in classical music, painting and folk arts such as Burra Katha, shadow puppet show, and Perini Shivatandavam, Gusadi Dance, Kolatam.

Kuntala Waterfalls in Adilabad

Monuments

Charminar, Golconda Fort, Qutb Shahi Tombs, Chowmahalla Palace, Falaknuma Palace, Birla Mandir and Nagarjun sagar, Bhongir Fort, Warangal Fort, Khammam Fort are some of the monuments in and around Hyderabad.

Religious destinations

Hindu worship destinations include Bhadrachalam Temple, Gnana Saraswati Temple, Yadagirigutta Temple, Ramappa Temple, Vemulawada Raja Rajeswara temple, the Thousand Pillar Temple.

There are religious worship centers of different religions in the state. These include Muslim worship destinations such as Makkah Masjid near Charminar, Khairtabad Mosque, Koh-e-qaim, Mian Mishk Masjid, Toli Masjid and Spanish Mosque.

Christian worship centers include the Diocese of Dornakal of the Church of South India, Bahe Church of South India, and Medak Cathedral. There are also some Buddhist destinations, such as Nelakondapalli, Dhulikatta, Phanigiri and Kolanpaka.

Telugu cinema

Telugu cinema, also known by its sobriquet as Tollywood, is a part of Indian cinema producing films in the Telugu language, and is centered in the Hyderabad, Telangana neighbourhood of Film Nagar. In the early 1990s, the Telugu film industry had largely shifted from Chennai to Hyderabad. The Telugu film industry is the second-largest film industry in India next to Bollywood Film Industry and followed by Tamil film industry Kollywood). In the years 2005, 2006 and 2008 the Telugu film industry produced the largest number of films in India, exceeding the number of films produced in Bollywood. The industry holds the Guinness World Record for the largest film production facility in the world.

Waterfalls

Kuntala Waterfall (45 metres (148 ft)) located in Kuntala, Adilabad district, is the highest waterfall in the state.

Bogatha Waterfall is waterfall located in Koyaveerapuram G, Wazeedu Mandal, Jayashankar Bhupalpally district, Telangana. It is located 120 kilometres (75 mi) from Bhadrachalam, 140 kilometres (87 mi) away from Warangal and 329 kilometres (204 mi) from Hyderabad.

Savatula Gundam Waterfalls are one of the many waterfalls located in Adilabad district, Telangana, India. They are located 30 km (19 mi) from Asifabad and 350 km (220 mi) from Hyderabad, the state capital.

Gowri Gundaala waterfalls at Sabitham village near Ramagundam in Peddapalli district.

CLOTHING AND FABRICS

The new state inherits one of the finest traditions in weaving and dying techniques as its cotton producing units (along with dye extraction) are famous in the world.

Saree is the most common clothing for women in Telangana even as langa voni, salwar kameez and churidaar are quite popular among unmarried women in the state.

Pochampally and Gadwal sarees are famous for their unique design, texture even as traders on the ancient silk route used to buy these merchandise as they were symbols of luxury and elegance at that time.

For men, dhoti (aka Pancha) is the traditional attire. But the Hyderabadi sherwani, the dress worn by the Nizams, is a ready fit on occasions like family ceremonies and gala functions.

Two types of cuisines in Telangana

Telangana has two types of food preparation - Telugu and Hyderabadi.

An extension of South Indian recipe, Telugu cuisine is made up of spicy food ingredients. Millet and roti dominate the meal variety along with jowar and bajra which feature most in the regular menu of a Telangana family.

Due to its proximity with Maharashtra, Chhattisgarh and northwest Karnataka, Deccan plateau foods have made inroads in Telangana menu table.

Telangana has some unique dishes such as jonna rotte (sorghum), sajja rotte (penisetum), or uppudi pindi (broken rice). A gravy or curry is called koora and pulusu (sour) in based on Tamarind. A deep fry reduction of the same is called vepudu. Kodi pulusu and mamsam (meat) vepudu are popular dishes in meat.

Telangana palakoora is a spinach dish cooked with lentils and eaten with steamed rice and rotis. Peanuts are added as special attraction and in Karimnagar district cashew nuts are added.

Sakinalu (aka Chakinalu), one of the most popular savouries in Telangana, is cooked during Makara Sankranti festival. This is a deep-fried snack made of rice flour, sesame seeds and flavoured with ajwain (carom seeds or vaamu in Telugu). These savouries are harder and spicier than the Telangana varieties.

An amalgamation of Persian, Mughlai, Telugu and Turkish cuisines, the Hyderabadi menu was developed by the Qutb Shahi dynasty and the Nizams. It has a mix of rice, wheat and meat dishes peppered with spices and herbs. The Hyderabadi cuisine has city specific specialties like Hyderabad (biryani and haleem), Aurangabad (Naan Qalia), Gulbarga (Tahari) and Bidar (Kalyani Biryani).

Dry coconut, tamarind and red chillies, besides spices, are the main ingredients that make Hyderabadi cuisine stand apart from north Indian recipes.

Architecture of Talangana

Kakatiyas built Thousand Pillar temple achieved new heights in architectural splendour.

Constructed by King Rudra Deva in 1163 CE, Thousand Pillar is a specimen of Kakatiyan style of the 12th century.

However, this majestic temple was destroyed by the invading Tughlaq dynasty from the north. Despite having thousand pillars, a devotee can have clear view of the god from any part of the temple without any hindrance.

Alampur style: All the nine temples in Alampur are dedicated to Lord Shiva and these structures dating back to 7th century CE were built by Badami Chalukyas who patronised art and architecture.

Despite the passage of centuries, these majestic temples exemplify the rich architecture of Telangana which amalgamated northern and western styles in temple construction.

However, they do not reflect the Dravidian style as is the case with Telangana state comprising coastal Telangana and Rayalaseema. The shikharas of these temples have a curvilinear form and are adorned with the miniature architectural devices. The plans and decoration similar to that of the rock cut temples.

The Alampur Navabhrama temples reflect adept skills in architecture and sculptural carvings.

Classical dance in Telangana

Called the 'dance of warriors', Perini Sivatandavam or just Perini Thandavam is an ancient dance form performed by males and has been revived in recent years. It is said that warriors used to enact this dance before the idol of Lord Siva while going to the battlefield during the rule of Kakatiyas.

The Kakatiya dynasty ruled Telangana and parts of Telangana for nearly two centuries with their capital in Warangal. This classical dance invokes 'Prerana' (inspiration) and is dedicated to Lord Shiva.

Carnatic music, folk arts

Kancherla Gopanna, popular as Bhakta Ramadasu or Bhadrachala Ramadasu, was a 17th century devotee of Lord Rama and a pioneer in composing ragas for the Carnatic music. He is one of the earliest vaggeyakaras (who compose both lyrics and sets them into musical style rendition) in Telugu language.

A number of folk songs had played vital role in the Telangana movement especially during the conduct of Dhoom Dham, a cultural event held as part of year-long statehood agitation. The state has a rich tradition in classical music, painting and folk arts such as burrakatha, shadow puppet show, and perini shiva tandavam, gusadi dance and kolatam.

Oggu Katha

A traditional folklore that renders songs in praise of Hindu gods Mallana, Beerappa and Yellamma by narrating their valiant deeds. This folklore is common among the Yadav and Karuma Golla communities who have dedicated themselves to singing ballads in praise of Lord Shiva, more popular as Mallikarjuna in Telangana regions.

Always on a journey, the community people narrate the stories of their caste gods in a ballad-style presentation earning the kudos of the audience. Two narrators transform themselves as mythological and legendary characters to enact a play-like rendition which makes Oggu Katha a lively ballad in Telangana.

Most of the singers worship Komrelly Mallanna temple as the presiding deity is their favourite and inspires them to carry on with their vocation.

Cultural treasure house

Museums in Hyderabad showcase the kingdoms of bygone era throwing light on some of the hidden facets of ancient civilisation of the Telangana region.

The Salar Jung Museum with collections from the huge property of the Salar Jung family is one of the three largest national museums of the country. Located at Darushifa on the southern banks of Musi river in Hyderabad, Salar Jung houses the biggest one-man collections of antiques in the world.

It is a well-known museum throughout India for its rare collections of artefacts, numismatics and invaluable objects of bygone eras that shed much light on the greatness of Indian civilisations.

The other museums are Nizam Museum, City Museum in Hyderabad and Birla Science Museum.

Tollywood

In terms of industry size and box office collections, Telugu films more popular as Tollywood are next only to Bollywood.

But Hyderabad has Ramoji Film City which is the world's largest production base for motion pictures. Also, with adoption of new techniques in film making, Telugu films are reaching out beyond their traditional markets.

Now overseas rights of Telugu films are being sold at exorbitant prices in the US, England, Malaysia and Singapore. At Ramoji Film City, a whole range of facilities for film shooting with a number of custom-built studios, production and film labs, among others, are offered under one integrated provider cutting down cost without compromising on quality.

Most of the south Indian language films are shot at this picturesque locale as the Film City goes the extra mile to woo producers and filmmakers for patronage.

Festivals of Telangana

Much grandeur and joy accompany festivals which are eagerly awaited by Telanganites. People visit temples, follow rituals at home and worship their favourite deities on religious occasions.

Some of the popular festivals are Ugadi, Dasara, Makara Sankranti, Guru Purnima, Sri Rama Navami, Hanuman Jayanti, Raakhi Pournami, Vinayaka Chaviti, Nagula Panchami, Krishnashtami, Deepavali, Mukkoti Ekadasi, Karthika Purnima and Ratha Saptami.

Regional festivals like Bonalu in Hyderabad, Batukamma (all over Telangana), Yedupayala Jatara in Medak and Sammakka Saralamma in Warangal district have thousands of followers with many flocking to these places on such occasion from neighbouring districts.

TELUGU CINEMA

Telugu cinema, also known by its sobriquet Tollywood, is the segment of Indian cinema dedicated to the production of motion pictures in the Telugu language, based in Hyderabad and Visakhapatnam, India. Since 1909, film maker Raghupathi Venkaiah Naidu was involved in producing short films and travelling to different regions in Asia to promote film work. In 1921, he produced the first Telugu silent film, *Bhishma Pratigna.* He is cited as the father of Telugu cinema. Tollywood is the second largest film industry in India.

In 1933, East India Film Company has produced its first Indian film, *Savitri* in Telugu. The film was based on a popular stage play by Mylavaram Bala Bharathi Samajam, directed by father of the "Telugu theatre Movement" Chittajallu Pullaiah and cast stage actors Vemuri Gaggaiah and Dasari Ramathilakam as "Yama" and "Savithri" respectively. The film was shot with a budget of estimated 1 million (US$14,000) in Calcutta. The blockbuster film has received an honorary diploma at the 2nd Venice International Film Festival.

The first film studio in South India, Durga Cinetone, was built in 1936 by Nidamarthi Surayya in Rajahmundry, Andhra Pradesh. The 1951 film *Patala Bhairavi* was the only South Indian film screened at the first India International Film Festival, held in Mumbai on 24 January 1952. CNN-IBN listed

Patala Bhairavi (1951), *Malliswari* (1951), *Devadasu* (1953), *Mayabazar* (1957), *Nartanasala*(1963), *Maro Charithra* (1978), *Maa Bhoomi* (1979), *Sankarabharanam* (1979), *Sagara Sangamam* (1983), and *Siva* (1989), among *The 100 Greatest Indian Films of All Time*. In the years 2005, 2006, 2008, and 2014 the industry has produced the largest number of films in India, exceeding the number of films produced in Bollywood.

The industry holds the Guinness World Record for the largest film production facility in the world, Ramoji Film City. The Prasads IMAX located in Hyderabad is one of the largest 3D IMAX screens, and the most attended cinema screen in the world. As per the CBFC report of 2014, the industry is placed first in India, in terms of films produced yearly. The industry holds a memorandum of understanding with the Motion Picture Association of America to combat video piracy. The *Baahubali (franchise)* produced by Tollywood studio Arka Media Works is the highest grossing Indian multilingual film of all time globally with a cumulative box office earnings of approximately 2,000 crore (US$280 million).

History

Early development

The Telugu film industry was originated with silent films in 1912, with the production and release of *Anusha Adusumalli* in 1921 The film was directed by Raghupathi Venkaiah Naidu and his son R. S. Prakash. On the other hand, Yaragudipati Varada Rao and, R. S. Prakash Rao have established a long-lasting precedent of focusing exclusively on religious themes; *Nandanar*, *Gajendra Moksham*, and *Matsyavatar*, three of their most noted productions, centred on religious figures, parables, and morals. In 1935, *Andhra Cine Tone* was built in Visakhapatnam by *Gottumukkala Jagannadha Raju*. He introduced digital theater sound with the 1935 film *Jagadamba*.

Rise of the "talkie"

The first Telugu film with audible dialogue, *Bhakta Prahlada*, was produced by H.M. Reddy, who directed the first

South Indian talkie Kalidas (1931). Bhakta Prahlada was completed on 15 September 1931, which henceforth became known as "Telugu Film Day" to commemorate its completion. Popularly known as talkies, films with sound quickly grew in number and popularity. In 1934, the industry saw its first major commercial success with *Lavakusa*. Directed by C. Pullaiah and starring Parupalli Subbarao and Sriranjani in lead roles, the film attracted unprecedented numbers of viewers to theatres and thrust the young industry into mainstream culture. By 1936, the mass appeal of film allowed directors to move away from religious and mythological themes. That year, under the direction of Krithiventi Nageswara Rao, *Prema Vijayam*, a film focusing on social issues, was released. Its success prompted the production of dozens of other immensely successful 'social films', notably 1939's *Vandemataram*, touching on societal problems like the practice of giving dowry, Telugu films increasingly focused on contemporary living: 29 of the 96 films released between 1937 and 1947 had social themes.

In 1938, Gudavalli Ramabrahmam, has co-produced and directed the social problem film, Mala Pilla which dealt with the crusade against untouchability, prevailing in pre-independent India. In 1939, He directed *Raithu Bidda*, starring thespian Bellary Raghava.

The film was banned by the British administration in the region, for depicting the uprise of the peasantry among the Zamindar's during the British raj. 1940 film, Viswa Mohini, is the first Indian film, depicting the Indian movie world. The film was directed by Y. V. Rao and scripted by Balijepalli Lakshmikanta Kavi, starring Chittor V. Nagaiah in the lead role. 1951 film Malliswari is the first Telugu film, to be screened at International film festivals like Asia Pacific Film Festival.

The film had a public release with thirteen prints along with Chinese subtitles at Beijing on 14, March 1953, and a 16 mm film print was also screened in the United States. The film was directed by Bommireddy Narasimha Reddy, a recipient of the Dada Saheb Phalke Award, and the Doctor of Letters honour.

The outbreak of World War II and the subsequent resource scarcity caused the British Raj to impose a limit on the use of filmstrip in 1943 to 11,000 feet, a sharp reduction from the 20,000 feet that had been common till then. As a result, the number of films produced during the war was substantially lower than in previous years. Nonetheless, before the ban, an important shift occurred in the industry: Independent studios formed, actors and actresses were signed to contracts limiting whom they could work for, and films moved from social themes to folklore legends. Ghantasala Balaramayya, has directed the mythological *Seetarama Jananam* under his home production, Prathiba Picture, marking veteran ANR's Telugu film acting debut in 1944.

Industry

Moola Narayana Swamy and B. N. Reddy founded Vijaya Vauhini Studios in 1948 in the city of Chennai. Indian film doyen L. V. Prasad, who started his film career with *Bhakta Prahlada*, founded Prasad Studios in 1956 based in Chennai. However, through the efforts of D. V. S. Raju, the Telugu film industry completely shifted its base from Chennai to Hyderabad in the early 1990s, during N. T. Rama Rao's political reign.

Veteran actor Akkineni Nageswara Rao relocated to Hyderabad and has developed Annapurna Studios. The Telugu film industry is one of the three largest film producers in India. About 245 Telugu films were produced in 2006, the highest in India for that year. Film studios in Hyderabad, developed by D. Ramanaidu and Ramoji Rao, are involved in prolific film production and employment. There is a fair amount of dispersion among the Indian film industries. Many successful Telugu films have been largely remade by the Bengali cinema and Hindi film industries.

The digital cinema network company UFO Moviez marketed by Southern Digital Screenz (SDS) has digitized several cinemas in the region. The Film and Television Institute of Telangana, Film and Television Institute of Andhra Pradesh, Ramanaidu Film School and Annapurna International School of Film and

Media are some of the largest film schools in India. The Telugu states consist of approximately 2800 theaters, the largest number of cinema halls of any state in India.

The Nandi Awards is the most prestigious award ceremony for excellence in the production of Telugu Film, Theatre and Television. It is presented annually at *Lalitha Kala Thoranam*in Hyderabad, by the Film, Television and Theatre Development Corporation *of the Telugu state(s). "Nandi" means "bull", the awards being named after the big granite bull at Lepakshi — a cultural and historical symbol of the Telugu culture.*

Commercial stance

Known for being commercially consistent, Telugu cinema had its influence over commercial cinema in India. As one of the revenue generating film industries, Telugu film production accounts for one percent of the gross domestic product of the region. The 1992 film Gharana Mogudu, directed by K. Raghavendra Rao, is the first Telugu film to gross over 10 crore at the box office.

The 2006 film *Bommarillu* was released worldwide with 72 prints. Owing to its success, the number of reels grew to about hundred. It collected a distributors share of 5 crore in its opening week in India. Released in six major metros in the United States, the film collected $73,200 (then approximately 0.3 crore) within the first four days of screening.

A 2006 survey conducted by a popular entertainment portal in the United States revealed that the film was watched by an Indian expatriate population of 65,000, which generated a revenue of 3 crore at that time. A cumulative gross revenue for the film was reported to be as 25 crore including 3.5 crore from overseas, the largest for any Telugu film at that time. Owing to this path breaking trade, the film was remade into Tamil, Bengali, Oriya and Urdu/Hindi. 2006 action film, *Pokiri* has been remade in Hindi, Tamil and Kannada in the following two years owing to the film's commercial success. It was screened at the IIFA film festival held in Dubai in 2006. Walt Disney

Pictures co-produced *Anaganaga O Dheerudu*, making it the first South Indian production by Disney.

The fantasy film *Magadheera* (2009) was released to critical acclaim; with a worldwide share of 78.1 crore (US$13 million) making it one of the highest grossing Telugu films of the time. The film was dubbed into Malayalam, Tamil and was remade in Bengali as *Yodha-The Warrior*, and emerged as a box office hit. 2011 action comedy, Dookudu was released among seventy nine screens in the US, the *Los Angeles Times* quoted it as *The biggest hit you've never heard of*. In the rest of north, east and west India, it opened up in 21 cities. The film set a box office record by collecting a gross of more than 1 billion at the time.

Eega (2012) grossed 1.25 billion (US$17 million) including all the dubbed versions. In 2013, Attarintiki Daredi collected a worldwide share of 492 million (US$8.2 million). The film collected a worldwide share of 798 million (US$13 million) in three weeks, becoming the biggest Telugu film grosser of all time. 2014 film's 1: Nenokkadine and Aagadu, became the highest opening weekend Indian film(s) in U.S. box office alongside Bollywood films like *Krrish 3* and *Kick*. Enhanced technology among live action animation, digital compositing, and special effects paved the way for upgrading from established cinematic norms. Visual effects based fantasy films like *Magadheera*, *Arundhati*, *Eega* and *Dhamarukam* emerged as blockbusters.

The 2015 epic film *Baahubali: The Beginning* received critical acclaim for its visual effects, production design, narration and background score. The film became the highest grossing Indian film within India, the third highest grossing Indian film globally, the first and only South Indian film to gross over 650 crore (6.5 billion) worldwide, the first non-Hindi film to gross over 100 crore (1 billion) in the dubbed Hindi version, and the highest grossing Telugu film of all time. The Beginning is nominated for Saturn Award for Best Fantasy Film by the American Academy of Science Fiction, Fantasy and Horror Films.

Critical reception

K. Viswanath

Vasiraju Prakasam and K. N. T. Sastry are one of the noted Indian film critics from the state. The industry is one of the largest producers of folklore, fantasy, mythological and melodrama films. Film makers like Kadiri Venkata Reddy, B. Vittalacharya and Kodi Ramakrishna have pioneered this genre. Mayabazar and Patala Bhairavi got critical acclaim at the inaugural International Film Festival of India in the 1950s. 1956 film Tenali Ramakrishna has garnered the All India Certificate of Merit for Best Feature Film. In 2013, IBN Live's Poll listed Mayabazar as the finest Indian film of all time.

Nartanasala won the best art direction award at the Afro Asian film festival in Jakarta. *Donga Ramudu* directed by K. V. Reddy was archived in the curriculum of the Film and Television Institute of India. Nammina Bantu received critical reception at the San Sebastián International Film Festival. 1967 film Ummadi Kutumbam was selected by Film Federation of India as one of its entries to the Moscow Film Festival. The 1968 cult classic Sudigundalu was screened at the Tashkent and Moscow Film Festivals.

Sankarabharanam won the Prize of the Public at the Besançon Film Festival of France in the year 1981. *Thilaadanam* won the New Currents Award at the 7th Busan International Film Festival of South Korea. B. Narsing Rao produced Maa Bhoomi which was showcased at Karlovy Vary Film Festival, Cairo and Sidney Film Festivals. He directed, *Daasi* and *Matti Manushulu* which won the Diploma of Merit award at the Moscow International Film Festival in 1989 and 1991 respectively. *Maa Ooru*directed by him won the Media Wave Award at the Hungary International festival of visual arts. In 2003, he directed Hari Villu which was nominated in the Critics' Week section at the 56th Cannes Film Festival. Cinematographer turned director, M. V. Raghu has directed the Neo-realistic film Kallu (1988), scripted by Gollapudi Maruti Rao has received thirty state awards and has garnered special mention from the CBFC Jury. Chandra Siddhartha's 1995 film, Nirantharam based on 1948 Telangana Rebellion, has received special mention at Cairo and Locarno International Film Festivals.

Bapu's directorial venture Sakshi was showcased at Tashkent International film festival in 1968. In 1976, He directed *Seeta Kalyanam* got critical acclaim at the BFI London Film Festival and Chicago International Film Festival, and is part of the curriculum at British Film Institute. *Swati Mutyam* (1986) is the only Telugu film to be sent by India as its official entry for the Best Foreign Language Film for the Academy Awards. *Swati Mutyam* and *Sagara Sangamam* got critical acclaim at Asia Pacific Film Festival.*Oka Oori Katha* has won special awards at Karlovy Vary International Film Festival and Carthage Film Festival. *Vanaja* won several international awards including the first prize in the live-action feature film category at the Chicago International Children's Film Festival. 2012 film Dream, has garnered the Royal Reel Award at the Canada International Film Festival.

2013 Fantasy film Eega has garnered awards for the *Most Original Film*, *Best Special Effects*, *Best Comedy*, *Best Fights*, *Best Film to watch with a crowd*, *Best Editing*, *Best Villain*and *Best Hero* (Fly) in the 8th Annual Edition Toronto After Dark Film Festival. 2013 Social problem film, Na Bangaaru Talli has received Best Film award at the Trinity International Film Festival in Detroit, and four Awards at the Indonesian International Film Festival. 2014 film Minugurulu was selected as *Best Indian Film* at the 9th *India International Children's Film Festival*, held at Bangalore. 2013 Cultural film, O Friend, This Waiting! has received special mention at the *Erasing Borders* Festival of Classical Dance, Indo-American Arts Council, New York, 2013. 2014 film *Parampara* has garnered the *Platinum Award for Best Feature* at the International Indonesian Movie Awards.

Cast and crew

Chittor V. Nagaiah was one of the most influential actors of South Indian cinema. Vemuri Gaggaiah, Kalyanam Raghuramaiah, R. Nageswara Rao, C.S.R. Anjaneyulu, Yadavalli Suryanarayana, C. H. Narayana Rao, Mudigonda Lingamurthy etc., are some of the finest method actors during the golden era. S. V. Ranga Rao, was one of the first south Indian actors to win the Best Actor Award for his portrayal of Kichaka in Nartanasala at the Indonesian Film Festival held in Jakarta. N. T. Rama Rao was one of the commercially successful Telugu actors of his time. K. N. T. Sastryand Pattabhirama Reddy have garnered international recognition for their pioneering work in Parallel Cinema. Adurthi Subba Rao, has garnered seven National Film Awards, for his pioneering work on drama films. Akkineni Kutumba Rao's *Patha Nagaramlo Pasivadu* received Cairo

International Film Festival's, Merit Certificate for best feature.

Dasari Narayana Rao has directed the most number of films in Telugu, he directed *Meghasandesam*, which got critical acclaim at Cannes and Moscow Film Festival. Noted director B. S. Narayana was a member of the Indian delegation to the *Tashkent Film Festival* in 1974, and the *Moscow International Film Festival* in 1975. V. N. Reddy, K. S. Prasad, and Jaya Krishna Gummadi one of the pioneering cinematographers in Telugu cinema, have garnered nationwide recognition for their work in cinematography in various Indian languages. His film *Tandra Paparayudu*(1986) starring Krishnam Raju was premiered at the 11th International Film Festival of India. Actor and producer, Krishna Ghattamaneni is credited with producing many technological firsts in Telugu film industry like the first Cinemascope film Alluri Seetharama Raju, first 70mm film*Simhasanam*, first DTS film *Telugu Veera Levara* (1988) and introducing cowboy and James Bond styles to the Telugu screen.

Relangi Venkata Ramaiah, and Ramana Reddy were a comedy double act during golden era. Emergence of director Jandhyala in the 1980s saw the growth of comedy film genre in Telugu cinema. Singeetam Srinivasa Rao and Ram Gopal Varma have received international recognition for bringing out new genres. Contemporary film maker's like Sekhar Kammula, Chandra Sekhar Yeleti, Mohan Krishna Indraganti, Deva Katta, G. Neelakanta Reddy and Narasimha Nandi have made their mark among the Indian panorama sections of the International Film Festival of India in the last decade. Noted film editor from the state, A. Sreekar Prasad, known for his initial works in Telugu films of the 1980s, has garnered national recognition for film editing across multiple languages of Indian cinema.

S. V. Ranga Rao, N. T. Rama Rao, Jaggayya, Kanta Rao, Bhanumathi Ramakrishna, Suryakantam, Gummadi, Savitri , Krishnam Raju and Sobhan Babu are the actors who received the erstwhile Rashtrapati Award for best performance in a leading role. Gummadi was an official member of the Indian delegation from South India to the *Tashkent Film Festival* in 1978 and 1982. He served as the Jury Member thrice for the 28th, 33rd, and 39th National Film Awards. Sri Sri was one of the influential film lyricists of his time, who garnered national honours like Sahitya Akademi Award, Best Lyricist and Soviet Land Nehru Award for his pioneering work.

Sharada, Archana, Vijayashanti, Rohini, Nagarjuna Akkineni, and P. L. Narayana are the actors to receive the National Film Award for best performance in acting. Chiranjeevi, widely known as Megastar, was listed among "The men who changed the face of the Indian Cinema" by IBN-liveIndia. Brahmanandam, a Telugu actor, holds a Guinness World Record for acting in the most films in the same language. Pete Draper, P. C. Sanath, Chakri Toleti and V. Srinivas Mohan are some of the visual effects professional's from the state known for their works in Telugu films.

Film Score

Susarla Dakshinamurthi, Parupalli Ramakrishnaiah Pantulu, Ogirala Ramachandra Rao, Pithapuram Nageswara Rao, Tanguturi Suryakumari, and Mangalampalli Balamuralikrishna are some of the influential music composers of Southern Indian cinema. Music composers such as Pendyala Nageswara Rao, R. Sudarshanam and R. Goverdhanam made contributions to folklore and mythological films.

Madhavapeddi Satyam, P. Adinarayana Rao, Gali Penchala Narasimha Rao, Chellapilla Satyam, P. B. Sreenivas, S. P. Kodandapani, G. K. Venkatesh, S. Hanumantha Rao, have contributed their work extensively for films containing themes of social relevance. S.P. Balasubrahmanyam is a multilingual playback singer from Telugu cinema to win National Film Awards across four languages. He holds the record of having recorded more songs than any other male playback singer and has received 25 state Nandi Awards.

S. Rajeswara Rao pioneered the use of light music in Telugu cinema; Rao's most rewarding assignments came from Gemini

Studios, which he joined in 1940 and with which he remained for a decade. Ghantasala, performed in the United States, England, and Germany. According to *The Hindu*, and *The Indian Express* he was "Such a divine talent and with his songs he could move the hearts of the people. Ghantasala's blending of classical improvisations to the art of light music combined with his virtuosity and sensitivity puts him a class apart, above all others in the field of playback singing". P. Susheela, has been recognized by both the *Guinness Book of World Records* and the *Asia Book of Records* for singing most number of songs in Indian languages. She is also the recipient of five National Film Award for Best Female Playback Singer and numerous state awards.

Works by S. Janaki, M. M. Keeravani, and Ramesh Naidu have received National recognition. Multi-instrumentalists duo Raj-Koti holds a notable career spanning a decade, the duo has garnered particular acclaim for redefining contemporary music. R. P. Patnaik is the current president of the Telugu Cine Music Association.

Distribution

As of 2012, *Dookudu* had one of the largest worldwide openings for a Telugu film, having been released globally onto 1,600 screens, including 71 in Hyderabad. The film became the first Telugu project to release in Botswana and was opened in a single screen with one show by the Telugu Association of Botswana. *Dookudu* was released over 79 theatres in the United States; the *Los Angeles Times* quoted *Dookudu* as "the biggest hit you've never heard of."

Further, it was released in Netherlands, Germany, South Africa, Dubai and Finland, the first for a Telugu film in addition to regular overseas markets such as Singapore, Malaysia and the UK. The producers approached the high court of India for a John Doe Order to prevent piracy of the film. It set a box office record for the Telugu film industry by collecting a gross of more than 1 billion (approximately 15.7 million US Dollars). The international version of *Baahubali: The Beginning* was released in China,

Japan, Korea, Taiwan, Indonesia, Thailand, Vietnam, Laos, Cambodia, Myanmar, Timor-Leste along with some European and Latin American countries.

Telugu film distribution territories

Territory name	Comprising areas
Nizam	Telangana State, Raichur and Koppal districts of Karnataka.
Ceded	Rayalaseema districts, Markapuram division of Prakasam district and Bellary district of Karnataka.
Vizag	Visakhapatnam, Srikakulam and Vizianagaram districts
East	East Godavari district.
West	West Godavari district.
Krishna	Krishna district.
Guntur	Guntur district and Ongole division of Prakasam district.
Nellore	Nellore district and Kandukur division of Prakasam district
Karnataka	Karnataka (except Raichur, Koppal and Bellary districts), Krishnagiri district of Tamil Nadu.
Tamil Nadu	Tamil Nadu (except Krishnagiri district).
Odisha	Odisha
Mumbai	Maharashtra, Gujarat and Goa.
Rest of India	other states of India

Amongst the above territories Nizam is considered by the distributors as having potential for maximum earnings with more than 50% of Tollywood revenue is generated only from the Nizam area. An additional territory known as overseas territory also exists where the maximum collection is from United States of America.

Guinness records

- Guinness Record had been awarded to Ramoji Film City,

Hyderabad as the largest film studio complex in the world, it opened in 1996 and measures 674 hectares (1,666 acres). With 47 sound stages, it has permanent sets ranging from railway stations to temples.

- D.Rama Naidu holds the Guinness World Record as the most prolific producer with 130 films.
- Dasari Narayana Rao holds the Guinness World Record as the most number of films directed with 151 films.
- Brahmanandam holds the Guinness World Record for acting in the most number of films in a single language, 1000+ films.
- S. P. Balasubramanyam holds the Guinness World Record for having sung the most number of songs for any male playback singer in the world, with the majority of his songs sung in Telugu.
- In 2002, the Guinness Book of Records named Vijaya Nirmala as the female director with the most number of films, having made 47 films. In a career spanning approximately two decades, she has acted in over 200 films with 25 each in Malayalam and Tamil and produced 15 films.
- In 2016, P.Susheela won guinness book of world record for singing highest number of songs for any female singer.

Dubbed films

The 1949 film *Keelu Gurram* was the first Telugu film to be dubbed into the Tamil language, being subsequently released under the name *Maya Kudhirai.* According to the Andhra Pradesh Film Chamber of Commerce, "as per the Judgement of Supreme Court in Ashirwad Films in W.P.(Civil) No.709 there will be no difference in taxation of films between the dubbed films coming in from other states and the films produced in the Telugu States".

FESTIVALS

Festivals are celebrated with much fervor and people used to go to temples on these days to offer special prayers.Some of the Festivals are Dasara, Bonalu, Eid ul fitr, Bakrid, Ugadi, Makara Sankranti, Guru Purnima , Sri Rama Navami, Hanuman Jayanti, Raakhi Pournami, Vinayaka Chaviti , Nagula Panchami, Krishnashtami, Deepavali,Mukkoti Ekadasi, Karthika Purnima and Ratha Saptami

Regional festivals

Telanganites not only celebrate the main festivals, but also celebrate certain regional festivals like Bonalu, Batukamma all over Telangana districts, Yedupayala Jatara in Medak, Sammakka Saralamma in Warangal district.

VISUAL ARTS

Paintings

Nirmal paintings are a popular form of painting done in Nirmal in Adilabad District.The paintings have golden hues. The region is well known for its Golconda and Hyderabad painting styles which are branches of Deccani painting. Developed during the 16th century, the Golconda style is a native style blending foreign techniques and bears some similarity to the Vijayanagara paintings of neighbouring Mysore. A significant use of luminous gold and white colours is generally found in the Golconda style.The Hyderabad style originated in the 17th century under the Nizams. Highly influenced by Mughal painting, this style makes use of bright colours and mostly depicts regional landscape, culture, costumes and jewellery.

Sculpture

Ramappa Temple:It lies in a valley at Palampet village of Venkatapur Mandal, in erstwhile Mulug Taluq of Warangal district, a tiny village long past its days of glory in the 13th-14th centuries. An inscription in the temple dates it to the year 1213 and said to have been built by a General Recherla Rudra, during the period of the Kakatiya ruler Ganapati Deva.

This medieval temple is a Shivalaya (where Shiva is worshipped) and named after the sculptor Ramappa. It is the only temple in the world named after its sculptor/architect. Its presiding deity, Ramalingeswara, is the form of Shiva and a personal god of the Avatar of Vishnu, Rama. The history says that it took 40 years to build this temple. Planned and sculpted by Ramappa, the temple was built on the classical pattern of being lifted above the world on a high star-shaped platform. Intricate carvings line the walls and cover the pillars and ceilings. Starting at its base to its wall panels, pillars and ceiling are sculpted figures drawn from Hindu mythology. The roof (garbhalayam) of the temple is built with bricks, which are so light that they are able to float on water.

Architecture

Carved pillar at Thousand Pillar Temple

Sangameshwar temple at Alampur

Alampur Temples:There are a total of nine temples in Alampur. All of them are dedicated to Shiva. These temples date back to the 7th century A.D and were built by the Badami Chalukyas rulers who were great patrons of art and architecture. Even after a time span of several hundred years, these grand temples still stand firm reflecting the rich architectural heritage of the country.

The temples are emblematic of the Northern and Western Indian styles of architecture. They do not reflect the Dravidian style of architecture as is generally common with the temples in this region.The *shikharas* of all these temples have a curvilinear form and are adorned with the miniature architectural devices. The plans and decoration similar to that of the rock cut temples.The Alampur *Navabhrama Temples* are historically important and reflect remarkable architectural skills.

Alampur was previously Known as *Halampuram*, *Hamalapuram* And *Alampuram*. Name of this place as

Hatampura, mentioned in the inscription dated *AD 1101* belongs to Western Chalukya

Kakatiya

The best examples of architecture under the Kakatiya dynasty (1163–1323) are the ruins of the Warangal Fort.

In The Thousand Pillar Temple is one of the very old temples of South India that was built by the kakatiyas. It stands out to be a masterpiece and achieved major heights in terms of architectural skills by the ancient kakathiya vishwakarma sthapathis.

It is believed that the Thousand Pillar Temple was built by King Rudra Deva in 1163 AD. The Thousand Pillar Temple is a specimen of the Kakatiyan style of architecture of the 12th century.

It was destroyed by the Tughlaq dynasty during their invasion of South India. It consists one temple and other building. There are one thousand pillars in the building and the temple, but no pillar obstructs a person in any point of the temple to see the god in the other temple.

Apart from Warangal, the Kakatiya dynasty constructed many hill forts forts including Golconda, Medak and Elgandal, and subsequent additions to these forts were made by the Bahmani and Qutb Shahi Sultanates.

Indo-Islamic

Early Indo-Islamic style of architecture is reflected in the monuments built by the Golconda Sultanate in Hyderabad. These include the Charminar, Golconda Fort and Qutb Shahi tombs.

Modern

During the reign of the Nizams of Hyderabad, European styled palaces and buildings became prevalent in the city of Hyderabad. Among the oldest surviving examples of architecture of this time is the Chowmahalla Palace, which showcases a diverse array of architectural styles, from the Baroque Harem to its Neoclassical royal court. The other palaces include Falaknuma Palace (inspired by the style of Andrea Palladio), Purani Haveli and King Kothi Palace all of which were built during the 19th century.

In the early 20th century, British Architect Vincent Esch was invited to Hyderabad by Asaf Jah VII.

He designed the Kachiguda railway station (1914), the High Court(1916), the City College (1920) and Osmania General Hospital (1921) in the Indo-Saracenic Revival style, which combines Indo-Islamic and European architectural styles.

Mandapam at Warangal Fort

Cultural sites

Salar Jung Museum, Hyderabad, Telangana established in 1951 is the largest collection of antiques of an individual in the world.

Telangana has many museums which depicts the culture of the erstwhile Kingdoms of the state.The Salar Jung Museum is an art museum located on the southern bank of the Musi river in the city of Hyderabad, Telangana, India. It is one of the three National Museums of India. The museum's collection was sourced from the property of the Salar Jung family.The Salar Jung Museum is the third largest museum in India housing the biggest one-man collections of antiques in the world. It is well known throughout India for its prized collections belonging to different civilizations dating back is very largest accocation to the 1st century.

The Telangana State Archaeology Museum in Hyderabad also houses a collection of rare Indian sculpture, art, artifacts as well as it's most prized exhibit, an Egyptian mummy. The other prominent Museums are Nizam Museum, Warangal Museum, City Museum, Hyderabad and Birla Science Museum.

Clothing

Telangana is the home to some of the finest historical cloth making/fashion and dying traditions of the world. Its rich cotton production, with its innovative plant dye extraction history stand next to its diamond mining. Traditional Women wear sari in the most parts of the state.Langa Voni, Shalwar kameez and Churidaar is popular among the Unmarried Women.

Some of the famous sarees made in Telangana are Pochampally Saree, Gadwal sari.Pochampally sarees have been popular since early 1800s. In 19th century popular with traders in the silk route which symbolised luxury and power. Found place in UNESCO tentative list of world heritage sites as part of 'iconic saree weaving clusters of India'.Pochampally saree received Intellectual Property Rights Protection or Geographical Indication (GI) status in 2005.

Male Clothing includes the traditional Dhoti also known as *Pancha* .The *Hyderabadi Sherwani* was the dress of choice of the Nizam of Hyderabad and Hyderabadi nobles. The Hyderabadi sherwani is longer than normal sherwani reaching below the knees. Sherwani is usually worn during the wedding ceremonies by the groom. A scarf called a dupatta is sometimes added to the sherwani.

Cuisine

Telangana has two types of cuisines, the Telugu cuisine and Hyderabadi cuisine. Telugu cuisine is the part of South Indian cuisinecharacterized by their highly spicy food. The Telangana state lies on the Deccan plateau and its topography dictates more milletand roti (leavened bread) based dishes. Jowar and Bajra features more prominently in their cuisine. Due to its proximity with Maharashtra, Chhattisgarh and northwest Karnataka, it shares some similarities of the Deccan plateau cuisine. The region has the spiciest food amongst all other Telugu and Indian cuisines.Telangana has some unique dishes in its cuisine, such as *jonna rotte*(sorghum), *sajja rotte* (penisetum), or *Uppudi Pindi* (broken rice). In Telangana a gravy or curry is called *Koora* and *Pulusu* (Sour) in based on Tamarind. A deep fry reduction of the same is called *Vepudu. Kodi pulusu* and *Mamsam (meat) vepudu* are popular dishes in meat. *Vankaya Brinjal Pulusu* or *Vepudu, Aritikaya Banana pulusu* or *Vepudu* are one of the many varieties of vegetable dishes. *Telangana palakoora* is a spinach dish cooked with lentils eaten with steamed rice and rotis. Peanuts are added as special attraction and in Karimnagar District, cashew nuts are added.

Sakinalu also called as *Chakinalu*, is one of the most popular savory in Telangana, is often cooked during Makara Sankrantifestival season. This a deep-fried snack made of rice flour, sesame seeds and flavoured with ajwain (carom seeds or vaamu in Telugu). These savories are harder and spicier than the Andhra varieties. Garijelu is a dumpling dish similar to the Maharashtrian karanji, which in Telangana is cooked with sweet stuffing or a savory stuffing with mutton or chicken kheema.

Hyderabadi cuisine, an amalgamation of Persian cuisine, Mughlai, Telugu, Turkish cuisines, developed by the Qutb Shahi dynastyand the Nizams of Hyderabad. It comprises a broad repertoire of rice, wheat and meat dishes and various spices and herbs.

Hyderabadi cuisine is the cuisine of the Hyderabadi Muslims, and an integral part of the cuisines of the former Hyderabad State that includes the state of Telangana and the regions of Marathwada (now in Maharashtra) and Hyderabad-Karanataka(now in Karnataka). The Hyderabadi cuisine contains city specific specialties like Hyderabad (Hyderabadi Biryani and Hyderabadi

Haleem) and Aurangabad (Naan Qalia), Gulbarga (Tahari), Bidar (Kalyani Biryani) and others. The use of dry coconut, tamarind, and red chillies along with other spices are the main ingredients that make Hyderabadi cuisine different from the North Indian cuisine

Performing arts

Dance

Perini Sivatandavam or *Perini Thandavam* is an ancient dance from Telangana which has been revived in recent times. It originated and prospered in Telanganaduring the Kakatiya dynasty.

The Perini Thandavam is a dance form usually performed by males. It is called 'Dance of Warriors'. Warriors before leaving to the battlefield enact this dance before the idol of Lord Siva.

The dance form, Perini, reached its pinnacle during the rule of the 'Kakatiyas' who established their dynasty at Warangal and ruled for almost two centuries. It is believed that this dance form invokes 'Prerana' (inspiration) and is dedicated to supreme dancer, Lord Siva.

Bonalu The folk festival of Bonalu in the Telangana region brings with it celebrations which see the colourfully dressed female dancers balancing pots (Bonalu), step to the rhythmic beats and tunes in praise of the village deity Mahankali. Male dancers called Potharajus precede the female dancers to the temple lashing whips and neem leaves adding colour to the festivity.

Music

Telangana has a diverse variation of Music from Carnatic Music to Folk music.Kancherla Gopanna, popularly known as Bhakta Ramadasu or Bhadrachala Ramadasu was a 17th-century Indian devotee of Rama and a composer of Carnatic music. He is one among the famous vaggeyakaras (a person who not only composes the lyrics but also sets them to music; vâk = word, speech; geya = singing, singable; geyakâra = singer) in the Telugu language.

The folk songs of Telangana had left a profound impact on the Statehood movement as it played a significant role in the success of the *Dhoom-Dham*, a cultural event that was a vital part of the agitations.

Oggu Katha

Oggu Katha or *Oggukatha* is a traditional folklore singing praising and narrating the stories of Hindu gods Mallana, Beerappa and Yellamma. It originated among the Yadav and Kuruma Golla communities, who devoted themselves to the singing of ballads in praise of Lord Shiva (also called Mallikarjuna). These tradition-loving and ritual-performing community moves from place to place, narrating the stories of their caste gods. Oggus are the traditional priests of the Yadavas and perform the marriage of Mallanna with Bhramaramba.

The narrator and his chorus i.e. two narrators-help in dramatizing the narration as very often, they transform themselves into two characters. The dramatization of the narrative is what gives the Oggu Katha its predominant place in the ballad tradition in Telangana, where Oggu Katha prevalent. The singers visit the shrine of Komrelly Mallanna Temple every year.

Cinema

Telugu cinema, also known by its sobriquet as *Tollywood*, is a part of Indian cinema producing films in the Telugu language, and is centered in the Hyderabad, Telangana neighbourhood of Film Nagar. The industry holds the Guinness World Record for the largest film production facility in the world, Ramoji Film City. The Prasads IMAX located in Hyderabad is one of the largest 3D IMAX screen, and the most attended cinema screen in the world. As per the CBFC report of 2012, the industry is placed second in India, in terms of films produced yearly.because of the film "Bahubali" casting Prabhas and Anushka.

QUALITY OF LIFE IN TELANGANA

One year after the formation of Telangana as the 29th state of Indian union on June 2, 2014, there is a mixed feelings among residents of Hyderabad along with a palpable fear that this region had missed out on core issues of social development and industrial growth. While there is confusion on administrative matters with the ruling party Telangana Rashtra Samithi (TRS) trying its best to allay the fears of the public on issues of employment and progress, it is a fact that the new state has not seen much change for better after its creation.

No doubt Hyderabad has been the showpiece metropolis having a large, skilled workforce and clusters of tech companies with rising income and social well-being which have given Telangana an opportunity to attract more investment from MNCs to this global city.

Need social infrastructure

But the rest of Telangana is crying for attention as more than 65% of the population are living in rural areas where employment crisis is putting question marks on the sustainable livelihood of thousands of youths who have no alternative but either go to other states or come to Hyderabad to eke out a decent living.

Moreover, the lack of higher educational institutes in Telangana districts has led to an emergence of a large pool of unskilled and semi-skilled youth who may find it very difficult to get jobs in a competitive city like Hyderabad.

Hence, TRS government has its task cut out in the coming years – creating employment and at the same time taking care of social development in the fields of education, healthcare and better support infrastructure across the state, all of which will ensure a better living standards for Telanganites.

Top among Indian cities

Hyderabad has been ranked top most among all other Indian

cities on quality of living, according to a survey by consulting firm Mercer which released its findings in March 2015.

Titled "Quality of Life 2015", the Mercer survey pointed out Indian cities had made very little progress when compared other cities of the world in terms of standards of living and other parameters.

While Hyderabad was ranked 138, Pune at 148, while Mumbai and New Delhi are ranked 152 and 154 respectively.

In the last few decades, Hyderabad has emerged as a city of choice due to factors such as improved options for international schools and choice of English-speaking schools. Moreover, the Rajiv Gandhi international airport at Shamshabad offers a wide range of global flights improving its connectivity thus improving its ranking on public services.

WHO has published a data on pollution around the world suggesting that 13 of the world's 20 most-polluted cities are all in India. This has impacted the overall scores of Indian cities in the Mercer survey.

A considerable jump in population in Mumbai and New Delhi had aggravated the existing problems, whereas Hyderabad is relatively safe with easy access to clean water, very little pollution and manageable traffic woes.

While the city has a range of international schools, its support infrastructure in terms of road connectivity, international airport and quality healthcare have made it a destination of choice for global investors who had spread out a vast tentacles of high tech industries and IT offices across the city.

Political bickering

Political rivalries and sabre rattling between Telangana and Andhra have hogged the media limelight with very little focus on improving the standards of living in both the sates.

A lot of groundwork has to be done to usher in development projects in rural Telangana where joblessness is rampant even as the unemployed youths are running out of options to secure a decent livelihood with steady source of income. It is noteworthy that the new industrial policy has assured project clearances at the earliest without any procedural delays or red tape.

While a number of incentives and sops are being doled out to woo investors, the state government on its part has to create the necessary support systems in terms of road connectivity, public institutions and better governance for ushering in speedy progress of Telangana.

3

Government and Politics

GOVERNMENT OF TELANGANA

Government of Telangana is a democratically elected body that governs the State of Telangana, India. The state government is headed by the Governor of Telangana as the nominal head of state, with a democratically elected Chief Minister as the real head of the executive. The governor who is appointed for five years appoints the chief minister and his council of ministers. Even though the governor remains the ceremonial head of the state, the day-to-day running of the government is taken care of by the chief minister and his council of ministers in whom a great deal of legislative powers is vested. The state government maintains its capital at Hyderabad and is seated at the Government Secretariator the Sachivalayam. The Government of Telangana was formed on 2 June 2014 after bifurcation of Andhra Pradesh as part of Andhra Pradesh Reorganisation Act, 2014.

GOVERNMENT AND ADMINISTRATION

Structure

The Governor is the constitutional head and the Chief Minister is head of the government who also heads the council of ministers. The Chief Justice of the high court is the head of the judiciary.

Governor

The Governor is appointed by the President for a term of five years. The executive and legislative powers lie with the Chief Minister and his council of ministers, who are appointed by the Governor. The Governors of the states and territories of India have similar powers and functions at the state level as that of the President of India at Union level. Only Indian citizens above 35 years of age are eligible for appointment. Governors discharge all constitutional functions such as the appointment of the Chief Minister, sending reports to the President about failure of constitutional machinery in a state, or with respect to issues relating to the assent to a bill passed by legislature, exercise or their own opinion.

Ekkadu Srinivasan Lakshmi Narasimhan has been the present governor since 2 June 2014. The Governor enjoys many different types of powers:

1. Executive powers related to administration, appointments, and removals.
2. Legislative powers related to lawmaking and the state legislature.
3. Discretionary powers to be carried out according to the discretion of the Governor.

Legislature

The legislature comprises the governor and the legislative assembly, which is the highest political organ in the state. The governor has the power to summon the assembly or to close the same. All members of the legislative assembly are directly elected, normally once in every five years by the eligible voters who are above 18 years of age.

The current assembly consists of 119 elected members and one member nominated by the governor from the Anglo-Indian Community. The elected members select one of its own members as its chairman who is called the speaker. The speaker is assisted by the deputy speaker who is also elected by the members. The conduct of meeting in the house is the responsibility of the Speaker.

The state assembly building in Hyderabad, Telangana.

The main function of the assembly is to pass laws and rules. Every bill passed by the house has to be finally approved by the governor before it becomes applicable.

The normal term of the legislative assembly is five years from the date appointed for its first meeting. But while a proclamation of state of emergency is in operation, the said period will be extended by Parliament by Laws for a period not exceeding one year at a time is waste government —

Judiciary

The High Court of Judicature at Hyderabad is the apex court for the state. It is a court of record and has all the powers of such a court including the authority to punish an individual for contempt of court. Like all other High Courts of India, this court also consists of a Chief Justice and other judges who are appointed by the President of India. Every judge including the Chief Justice is appointed by the President of India by Warrant under his hand and seal. Every permanent and additional judge will continue in office until the age of 62

The High Court of Telangana is located in Hyderabad, Telangana and there are courts in every district centers and some municipal centers.

Executive

Like in other Indian states, the Executive arm of the state is responsible for the day-to-day management of the state. It consists of the Governor, the Chief Minister and the Council of Ministers.

The secretariat headed by the secretary to the governor assists the council of ministers. The council of ministers consists of cabinet ministers, ministers of state and deputy ministers. The chief minister is assisted by the chief secretary, who is the head of the administrative services.

Chief Minister

KCR,Incumbent Chief Minister of Telangana

The executive authority is headed by the Chief Minister of Telangana, who is the de facto head of state and is vested with most of the executive powers; the Legislative Assembly's majority party leader is appointed to this position by the Governor. The present Chief Minister is Kalvakuntla Chandrashekar Rao, who took office on 2 June 2014. Generally, the party which reaches more than half mark i.e. 60 seats out of 119 decides the Chief Minister.

Council of Ministers

The Council of Ministers, which answers to the Legislative Assembly, has its members appointed by the Governor; the appointments receive input from the Chief Minister. They are collectively responsible to the legislative assembly of the State. Generally, the winning party and its chief minister chooses the ministers list and submit the list for the Governor's approval.

Administrative divisions

Telangana State has been divided into 31 districts. The business of the state government is transacted through the various secretariat departments based on the rules of business. Each department consists of secretary to government, who is the official head of the department and such other undersecretaries, junior secretaries, officers, and staffs subordinate to him/her. The *Chief secretary* superintending control over the whole secretariat and staff attached to the ministers.

Elections

Elections to the state assembly are held every five years. Elections are generally held for Parliament, State assembly and regional panchayats. Like all other Indian states, the minimum age of registration of a voter is 18 years.

Election Commission announced dates for elections in five states including Madhya Pradesh, Rajasthan, Telangana, Chhattisgarh and Mizoram. Polls in Telangana, Rajasthan on Dec 7, results on Dec 11: EC

GOVERNMENT AND POLITICS

Telangana is governed by a parliamentary system of representative democracy, a feature the state shares with other Indian states. Universal suffrage is granted to residents. There are three branches of government.

1. Executive authority is vested in the Council of Ministers headed by the Chief Minister, although the titular head of government is the Governor. The Governor is the head of state appointed by the President of India. The leader of the party or coalition with a majority in the Legislative Assembly is appointed as the Chief Minister by the Governor, and the Council of Ministers are appointed by the Governor on the advice of the Chief Minister. The Council of Ministers reports to the Legislative Assembly.
2. The legislature, the Telangana Legislative Assembly and the Telangana Legislative Council, consists of elected members and special office bearers such as the Speaker and Deputy Speaker, that are elected by the members. Assembly meetings are presided over by the Speaker or the Deputy Speaker in the Speaker's absence. The Assembly is bicameral with 119 Members of the Legislative Assembly and 40 Member of the Legislative Council. Terms of office run for 5 years unless the Assembly is dissolved prior to the completion of the term. The Legislative Council is a permanent body with one-third members retiring every two years.
3. The judiciary is composed of the High Court of Judicature at Hyderabad and a system of lower courts.

Auxiliary authorities known as *panchayats*, for which local body elections are regularly held, govern local affairs. The state contributes seats to Lok Sabha.

The main players in the regional politics are the Telangana Rashtra Samithi, All India Majlis-e-Ittehadul Muslimeen, Telugu Desam Party, Bharatiya Janata Party and Indian National Congress. Following the Telangana Legislative

Assembly Election in 2014, the Telangana Rashtra Samithi under Kalvakuntla Chandrashekar Rao was elected to power.

ANDHRA PRADESH REORGANISATION ACT, 2014

The Andhra Pradesh Reorganisation Act, 2014, popularly known as the Telangana Act is an Act of Indian Parliament that bifurcated the state of Andhra Pradesh into Telangana and the residuary Andhra Pradesh state, due to the Telangana movement. The Act defined the boundaries of the two states, determined how the assets and liabilities were to be divided, and laid out the status of Hyderabad as the permanent capital of new Telangana state and temporary capital of the Andhra Pradesh state.

An earlier version of the bill, *Andhra Pradesh Reorganisation Act, 2013*, was rejected by the Andhra Pradesh Legislative Assembly on 30 January 2014. The 2014 bill was passed in the Lok Sabha on 18 February 2014 and in the Rajya Sabha on 20 February 2014.The bill was attested by the President of India, Pranab Mukherjee on 1 March 2014 and published in the official Gazette on 2 June 2014 which is also the 'appointed day' according to the act. The new states were created on 2 June 2014.

Legislative history

The Union Cabinet formed a Group of Ministers (GoM) committee in August 2013 led by the Union Home Minister, Sushil Kumar Shinde to look into the suitability of a division of Andhra Pradesh. The members included the Finance Minister, P. Chidambaram, Health Minister Ghulam Nabi Azad, Petroleum Minister & Natural Gas Minister Veerappa Moily, Union Rural Development Minister Jairam Ramesh and minister of state in PMO Narayanaswamy. It also took the Srikrishna committee on Telangana into account.

A duly validated no-confidence motion against the Congress government was submitted to the speaker of the house Meira Kumari by Congress MPs from Andhra Pradesh making the sitting government a minority government. Long held parliamentary procedure that required immediate consideration of no-confidence motions intended to prevent illegitimate governments from passing laws was ignored by the speaker. Amidst a lot of protest in the Lok Sabha (the lower house of the Parliament of India), the bill was introduced by the speaker Meira Kumar at 12:00 pm on 13 February 2014. During this time, there was a lot of shouting of slogans and disruption of proceedings by the Seemandhra (non-Telangana) MPs in the parliament who were determined to stop the bill. The Indian National Congress party MP's attacked the anti-Telangana protestors, and the MP Lagadapati Rajagopal used pepper spray in the parliament. Later he said he was attacked by some Congress MPs from other states and had to use it in self-defense. The parliament was then adjourned at 12:05 pm to 02:00 pm.

The leader of the opposition in the Lok Sabha Sushma Swaraj said she did not know if the bill was introduced. On 18 February 2014, the Telangana Bill was passed by the Voice Vote in the Lok Sabha with support from the Bharatiya Janata Party (BJP) while the live telecast of the House was cut off and the doors and galleries were sealed. The Seemandhra leaders accused the United Progressive Alliance government of having taken it up for electoral gains and said it was a "black day" for the Indian parliament.

On 20 February, the Telangana bill was passed by the Rajya Sabha (the higher house of parliament) with support from the BJP. MPs from various parties asked for division but it was rejected by the speaker. Finally, the bill was passed by a voice vote.

The bill received the assent of the President and published in the Gazette on 1 March 2014. The new State came into effect "from the date set by the central government also known as appointed date." It became the 29th state of India.

Suspension of members of parliament

Due to disruptions to the House, Meira Kumar suspended 18 MPs from Andhra Pradesh on 13 February 2014 for the rest of the session. They included 11 MPs of the Congress party (Sabbam Hari, Anantha Venkatarami Reddy, Rayapati Sambasiva Rao, S. P. Y. Reddy, M. Sreenivasulu Reddy, V. Aruna Kumar, A. Sai Prathap, Suresh Kumar Shetkar, K. R. G. Reddy, Bapi Raju Kanumuri and G. Sukhender Reddy), three MPs of the Telugu Desam party (Niramalli Sivaprasad, Nimmala Kristappa, and K. Narayana Rao), two MPs of YSR Congress (Y. S. Jaganmohan Reddy and M. Rajamohan Reddy), and two other MPs from the Telangana region.

Resolution for the united Andhra Pradesh in Assembly

Though only an opinion is required under Article 3 of the Indian Constitution, a resolution was adopted and the bill was rejected by the Andhra Pradesh Legislative Assembly and Council on 30 January 2014. It is to be noted that only 119 out of 294 MLAs in state assembly are from Telangana. Non-Telangana MLAs opposed the bill. This was the first instance a state was re-organized after a state clearly expressed an opinion against the re-organization in Indian history.

Petitions against the Bill in Supreme Court

Nine petitions were filed in the Supreme Court of India requesting a stay of the tabling of the Andhra Pradesh Reorganisation Bill in parliament. The court rejected the pleas saying, "We do not think this is the appropriate stage for us to interfere". They would only consider the petition if the bill was passed in parliament. But the court issued notices to the centre regarding the issue on 7 March 2014. The apex court would take up the issue on 5 May 2014. The next hearing in the Supreme Court was scheduled for 20 August 2014 One petitioner approached the Supreme Court praying that the parliament does not have the power either under Articles 3, 4(2) or any other provision of the Constitution of India to divide a state except by an appropriate amendment of the Constitution under article 368 and with the unanimous consent of the people of the affected State or States.While invoking Articles 2 & 3, the deemed constitutional amendment provision under article 4 (2) of the constitution bypassing Article 368 was said to be invalid after the 24th amendment in 1971. The law ministry of the union government considered bringing appropriate amendments (including constitutional amendments) to the Act to bring legality to it.

The common high court of Andhra Pradesh and Telangana states stated that the division of the high court located at Hyderabad can only be done with the formation of separate high court for Andhra Pradesh located in that state as per section 31 of the Act. A separate high court for Telangana can not be formed by dividing the present common high court as the existing high court at Hyderabad would become high court of Telangana state after the formation of one for Andhra Pradesh.

On the applicability of the section 47 of Andhra Pradesh Reorganisation Act, 2014, Supreme Court in its judgement clarified the manner the financial assets and liabilities of undivided state departments and corporations are to be shared between the new states.

In an effort to avoid the huge financial burden to finance the creation of many institutions in the truncated AP state, the affidavit of central government clinched the dispute against the Telangana state AP state also decided to approach Supreme Court regarding the discriminatory sharing of commercial taxes income and refunds under sections 50, 51 and 56 of the act. The state is weary of centres inaction for a long time to amend these sections such that AP state would not loose INR 36 billions.

Details of the Bill

The bill was introduced on 5 December 2013, the first day of the winter session in the Legislative Assembly of Andhra Pradesh. The Union cabinet approved formation of Telangana with ten districts. Hyderabad will remain as the common capital under the Governor's supervision for not more than ten years. A new capital city for Andhra Pradesh would be declared in 45 days.

The Bill was drafted based on the boundaries of the proposed Telangana State as approved by the Union Cabinet in its meeting on 3 October 2013. The new state of Telangana would have 119 elected members of its legislative assembly, 40 members of its legislative council, 17 members of the Lok Sabha and 7 members in the Rajya Sabha. The residuary state of Andhra Pradesh would have 175 elected MLAs, 50 MLCs, 25 MPs of Lok Sabha and 11 MPs of Rajya Sabha.

There would be a common High Court and its expenditure would be apportioned between the two successor states based on population ratio until a separate court was set up under Article 214 for the residuary state of Andhra Pradesh. The existing Public Service Commission would be the Public Service Commission for the residuary state of Andhra Pradesh and the Union Public Service Commission would, with the approval of President, act as the Public Service Commission for Telangana.

The Ministry of Water Resources of the Government of India would constitute a Krishna River Management Board and a Godavari River Management Board within a period of 60 days from the date of coming into force of the Andhra Pradesh Reorganisation Bill. The Boards would be responsible for the administration, regulation and maintenance of the head works of the dams, reservoirs or head works of canals, as notified by the Government of India on Krishna and Godavari rivers, to implement all the awards made by the Tribunals. The Boards would be responsible for making an appraisal of proposals for construction of new projects on Krishna and Godavari rivers and give technical clearance. While not agreeing for the fresh water allocation of Krishna river among all the four riparian states, the extented Justice Brijesh Kumar tribunal ruled that the water sharing between Andhra Pradesh and Telangana states would be finalised project wise from the water allocations made to erstwhile Andhra Pradesh state by earlier Bachawat tribunal. It also stated that the primary reason for the division of the erstwhile state was to "fulfil the political and democratic aspirations of the people of Telangana region," and not inequitable sharing of water.

The Governor shall have special responsibility to the security of life, liberty and property of all those who reside in the common capital of Hyderabad. The Governor's responsibility shall extend to matters such as law and order, internal security and safety of all vital installations in the discharge of these functions. This transitory provision shall cease to have effect after a period not exceeding 10 years.

The Bill provides for the creation of separate cadres of All India Services in respect of the two states from the appointed day. Advisory Committee(s) would be constituted to ensure fair and equitable treatment of all employees.

The Government of India shall help the successor states of Telangana and Andhra Pradesh in raising additional police forces for maintenance of public order and shall also deploy one additional unit of the force in Hyderabad for a period of five years.

The Greyhound training centre in Hyderabad shall function as common training centre for the successor states for three years. In this period of three years, the GoI shall assist the successor state of Andhra Pradesh in setting up a similar training centre for Greyhounds. The existing Greyhound and OCTOPUS forces shall be distributed between the two states.

Of the total equity of Singareni Collieries Company Limited (SCCL), 51 per cent shall be with Government of Telangana and 49 per cent with Government of India. Existing coal linkages of SCCL shall continue without any change. New linkages shall be allotted to the successor States as per the new coal distribution policy by the Government of India.

Allocation of natural gas will continue to be done as per the policies and guidelines issued by the Government of India. The royalties payable on domestic on-shore production of oil and gas shall accrue to the state in which such production takes place. Allocation of power from Central generating stations shall be allocated to the successor states in the ratio of the average of the actual energy consumption of last five years of the relevant Discoms. For a period of 10 years, the successor state that has a deficit of electricity shall have the first right of refusal for the purchase of surplus power from the other state.

Later Polavaram ordinance merging the project-affected villages in the residuary Andhra Pradesh state was accepted by the Parliament in July 2014. Seven mandals from Khammam district of Telangana have been transferred to Andhra Pradesh. Four mandals from Bhadrachalam revenue division namely, Chinturu, Kunavaram, Vararamachandrapuram, Bhadrachalam (excluding the Bhadrachalam revenue village) were transferred to East Godavari district. Three mandals from Palvancha revenue division namely, Kukunoor, Velerupadu, Burgampadu (except 12 villages namely, pinapaka, morampalli, banjara, burgampadu, naginiprolu, krishnasagar, tekula, sarapaka, iravendi, motepattinagar, uppusaka, nakiripeta and sompalli), have been added to West Godavari district. This came into force as the 16th Lok Sabha has passed the Polavaram Ordinance Bill with the voice vote on 11 July 2014.

New capital for residual Andhra Pradesh

On 4 September 2014, the Chief Minister of Andhra Pradesh Nara Chandrababu Naidu, declared in the Legislative Assembly that the new capital of Andhra Pradesh state would come up in and around in between Guntur and Vijayawada. The capital city was named as Amaravati on 1 April 2015.

POLITICS OF TELANGANA

The President issued a gazette notification that Telangana state will be carved out of Andhra Pradesh on 2 June 2014.

Telangana movement

In the early Telangana movement, Marri Chenna Reddy formed a party call *Telangana Praja Samiti* to lead the Telangana movement. In November 1969, there was a major split in the party and as result the movement went down. After 2 years the Telangana Praja Samiti was dissolved and its members rejoined the Congress. On 29 November 2009, KCR started a fast-unto-death, demanding that the Congress party introduce a Telangana bill in Parliament. Student organisations, employee unions, and various organisations joined the movement.

As general strikes shut down of Telangana, Telangana Bill was passed in Lok Sabha on 18 February 2014 and in Rajya Sabha on 18 February 2014 with the support form the BJP. On 4 March 2014 the Government of India declared that 2 June would be the Telangana Formation Day.

4

Language and Literature

LANGUAGES

About 76% of the population of Telangana speak Telugu, 12% speak Urdu, and 12% speak other languages. Before 1948, Urdu was the official language of Hyderabad State, and due to a lack of Telugu-language educational institutions, Urdu was the language of the educated elite of Telangana.

After 1948, once Hyderabad State joined the new Republic of India, Telugu became the language of government, and as Telugu was introduced as the medium of instruction in schools and colleges, the use of Urdu among non-Muslims decreased.

LITERATURE

Muhammad Quli Qutb Shah was the first Saheb-e-dewan of Urdu. Other poets of Telangana from the early era include Pothana, Kancherla Gopanna or Bhakta Ramadasu, Malliya Rechana, Gona Budda Reddy, Palkurthi Somanatha, Mallinâtha Sûri, and Hulukki Bhaskara.

In the modern era poets include such figures as Padma Vibhushan Kaloji Narayana Rao, Sahitya Akademi Award recipient Daasarathi Krishnamacharyulu, and Jnanpith Award recipient C. Narayana Reddy, as well as P. V. Narasimha Rao, ninth Prime Minister of India. Samala Sadasiva was selected for the Kendra Sahitya Puraskaram distinction.

His book *Swaralayalu* on the subject of Hindustani classical music won the award for the year 2011.

5

Geography and Flora & Fauna

GEOGRAPHY

Telangana is situated on the Deccan Plateau, in the central stretch of the eastern seaboard of the Indian Peninsula. It covers 112,077 square kilometres (43,273 sq mi). The region is drained by two major rivers, with about 79% of the Godavari River catchment area and about 69% of the Krishna River catchment area, but most of the land is arid. Telangana is also drained by several minor rivers such as the Bhima, the Maner, the Manjira and the Musi.

The annual rainfall is between 900 and 1500 mm in northern Telangana and 700 to 900 mm in southern Telangana, from the southwest monsoons. Various soil types abound, including chalkas, red sandy soils, dubbas, deep red loamy soils, and very deep black cotton soils that facilitate planting mangoes, oranges and flowers.

Climate

Telangana is a semi-arid area and has a predominantly hot and dry climate. Summers start in March, and peak in May with average high temperatures in the 42 °C (108 °F) range. The monsoon arrives in June and lasts until September with about 755 mm (29.7 inches) of precipitation. A dry, mild winter starts in late November and lasts until early February with little humidity and average temperatures in the 22–23 °C (72–73 °F) range.

Ecology

The Central Deccan Plateau dry deciduous forests ecoregion covers much of the state, including Hyderabad. The characteristic vegetation is woodlands of *Hardwickia binata* and *Albizia amara*. Over 80% of the original forest cover has been cleared for agriculture, timber harvesting, or cattle grazing, but large blocks of forest can be found in Nagarjunsagar-Srisailam Tiger Reserve and elsewhere. The more humid Eastern Highlands moist deciduous forests cover the Eastern Ghats in the eastern part of the state.

National Parks and Sanctuaries

Telangana has three National Parks: Kasu Brahmananda Reddy National Park in Hyderabad district, and Mahavir Harina Vanasthali National Park and Mrugavani National Park in Ranga Reddy district.

Indian peafowl (**Pavo cristatus**) *near Hyderabad*

Wildlife Sanctuaries in Telangana include Eturunagaram Wildlife Sanctuary and Pakhal Wildlife Sanctuary in Warangal District, Kawal Tiger Reserve and Pranahita Wildlife Sanctuary in Adilabad district, Kinnerasani Wildlife Sanctuary in Khammam district, Manjira Wildlife Sanctuary in Medak district,

Nagarjunsagar-Srisailam Tiger Reserve in Nalgonda and Mahbubnagar districts, Pocharam Wildlife Sanctuary in Medak and Nizamabad districts, Shivaram Wildlife Sanctuary in Karimnagar district.

Sacred groves are small areas of forest preserved by local people. Sacred groves provide sanctuary to the local flora and fauna. Some are included within other protected areas, like Kadalivanam in Nagarjunsagar–Srisailam Tiger Reserve, but most stand alone. There are 65 sacred groves Telangana—two in Adilabad district, thirteen in Hyderabad district, four in Karimnagar district, four in Khammam district, nine in Mahbubnagar district, four in Medak district, nine in Nalgonda district, ten in Ranga Reddy district, and three in Warangal district.

TELANGANA GEOGRAPHY

Situated on the Deccan plateau, Telangana state occupies 1.14 lakh sq km on the central stretch of the eastern seaboard of the Indian peninsula.

Despite the region drained by two major rivers - 69% of Krishna's catchment areas and 79% of Godavari - most of the land is dry and arid. There are also minor rivers like Bhima, Manjira and Musi that crisscross the state comprising 10 districts in all.

The annual rainfall ranges from 900 to 1,500 mm in northern Telangana and 700 to 900 mm in southern Telangana, mostly getting the precipitation from the southwest monsoon.

Various soil types are found in Telangana - chalkas, red sandy soils, dubbas, deep red loamy soils, and very deep b.c.soils - that facilitate planting mangoes, oranges and flowers.

It is noteworthy that 45% of forest cover of undivided Andhra is now located in the five districts of Telangana.

Much of its area is occupied by the Telangana plateau in the north and the Golconda plateau in the south and is composed of gneissic rock.

The plateau's average elevation is about 1,600 feet with its peaks in the west and southwest and gradually sloping down towards the east and northeast, where it meets the disjointed ridges of the Eastern Ghats ranges.

Climate in Telangana

The summer begins from March to end in June, followed by a period of tropical rains from July to September; and finally, winter occurs from October to February.

Summers are very warm to extreme hot and dry, with temperatures often crossing 42-43 degree Celsius.

The annual precipitation mostly from the rainy southwest monsoon winds varies across the state. It averages about 35 inches (900 mm) per year, although the annual total often varies considerably from the average and can be as little as 20 inches (500 mm) in drier areas.

The average minimum temperatures in Hyderabad reach about 15 degree Celsius in January and February, while in the elevated areas it falls between 10 and 12 degree Celsius in the winter.

Vegetation in Telangana

While thorny vegetation is spread across the hills of the plateau region, thick jungles are common in the northeast along and near the Godavari river.

Comprising one-fourth of land area, the forests are both moist deciduous and dry savannah in nature with teak, rosewood, wild fruit trees and bamboos found in plenty.

Generally, neem, banyan, mango and papal trees are quite common across Telangana districts.

Some of the wildlife spotted in the reserve forests are tigers, blackbucks, hyenas, sloth bears, gaurs and chital which thrive in a symbiotic ecology prevalent in the Telangana forests.

Home to two dozen national parks, wildlife sanctuaries and reserve forests, Telangana has thousands of bird species including flamingos and pelicans.

ADMINISTRATIVE DIVISIONS

The state is divided into 31 districts which are further divided into 68 revenue divisions and they are in turn divided into 584 mandals.

The districts in the state are

- Adilabad
- Bhadradri Kothagudem
- Hyderabad
- Jagtial
- Jangaon
- Jayashankar Bhupalpally
- Jogulamba Gadwal
- Kamareddy
- Karimnagar
- Khammam
- Komaram Bheem Asifabad
- Mahabubabad
- Mahbubnagar
- Mancherial
- Medak
- Medchal Malkajgiri
- Nagarkurnool
- Nalgonda
- Nirmal
- Nizamabad
- Peddapalli
- Rajanna Sircilla
- Ranga Reddy
- Sangareddy
- Siddipet
- Suryapet
- Vikarabad

- Wanaparthy
- Warangal Rural
- Warangal Urban
- Yadadri Bhuvanagiri

There are a total of 12 cities which include 6 municipal corporations and 38 municipalities. Hyderabad is the only million-plus populated city in the state.

TELANGANA FOREST DEPARTMENT

Telangana Forest Department(Telugu: $F2>#□5@□6>□) is one of the administrative divisions of the government of Telangana. It is headed by the Principal Chief Conservator of Forests. The primary function of this department is protection, conservation and management of forests in Telangana State. It concerns on the entity of the human beings with the survival of each species in its habitat.

FLORA AND FAUNA

Telangana, located strategically in the central region of the Indian sub-continent, has representatives of Indian plant and animal life. The vegetation found in the state is largely of dry deciduous type with a mixture of teak, and species of the genera Terminalia, Pterocarpus, Anogeissus etc.The varied habitat harbors a diversity of fauna which includes tiger, panther, wolf, wild dog, hyena, sloth bear, Gaur, Black Buck, Chinkara, Chowsingha, Nilgai, Cheetal, Sambar and a number of birds and reptiles in the forest.etc

Objectives

The overall objective of the Telangana Forest Department is to conserve biodiversity and eco-systems of forests and wilderness areas to ensure water security and food security of the state. Wildlife and wildlife habitats should be conserved and sustainably managed to meet the social, economic, ecological, cultural, recreational and spiritual needs of the present and future generations of people in the state.

Haritha Haram

The government has launched a scheme, Haritha Haram, to make entire Telangana green.Telangana government has decided to launch a massive tree plantation programme to bring entire Telangana under green cover in the next three years.It is estimated that the entire Telangana state requires 210 crore saplings to bring 33 per cent of the area under green cover.

Management

The Forest Department is organised in an administrative hierarchy ranging from Principal Chief Conservator of Forests to Forest Watchers, Mahouts and others.

Principal Chief Conservator of Forests

The Principal Chief Conservator of Forests (PCCF) is in overall control of the whole Forest Department. All significant orders, permissions, declarations and authorisations of the department are personally reviewed, approved and signed by him.

6

Economy

ECONOMY OF TELANGANA

The economy of Telangana is mainly supported by agriculture. Two important rivers of India, the Godavari and Krishna, flow through the state, providing irrigation. Farmers in Telangana mainly depend on rain-fed water sources for irrigation. Rice is the major food crop. Other important local crops are cotton, sugar cane, mango and tobacco. Recently, crops used for vegetable oil production, such as sunflower and peanuts, have gained favour. There are many multi-state irrigation projects in development, including Godavari River Basin Irrigation Projects.

The state has also started to focus on the fields of information technology and biotechnology. Telangana is one of top IT exporting states of India. There are 68 Special Economic Zones in the state.

Telangana is a mineral-rich state, with coal reserves at Singareni Colleries.

Economy

The economy of Telangana is mainly driven by agriculture. Two important rivers of India, the Godavari and Krishna, flow through the state, providing irrigation. Farmers in Telangana mainly depend on rain-fed water sources for irrigation. Rice is the major food crop. Other important crops are cotton, sugar cane, mango and tobacco. Recently, crops used for vegetable oil production such as sunflower and peanuts have gained favour. There are many multi-state irrigation projects in development, including Godavari River Basin Irrigation Projects and Nagarjuna Sagar Dam, the world's highest masonry dam.

Coal Handling Ropeway near Aswapuram, Khammam district

The state has also started to focus on the fields of information technology and biotechnology. Telangana is one of top IT-exporting states of India. There are 68 Special Economic Zones in the state.

Telangana is a mineral-rich state, with coal reserves at Singareni Collieries Company.

Agriculture

Paddy fields in Warangal district

Rice is the major food crop and staple food of the state. Other important crops are maize, tobacco, mango, cotton and sugar cane.Agriculture has been the chief source of income for the state's economy. The Godavari and Krishna rivers flow through the state, providing irrigation. Apart from major rivers, there are small rivers like Tunga Bhadra, Bima, Dindi, Kinnerasani, Manjeera, Manair, Penganga, Pranahitha, peddavagu and Taliperu. There are many multi-state irrigation projects in development, including Godavari River Basin Irrigation Projects and Nagarjuna Sagar Dam, the world's highest masonry dam.

Agri Export Zones for the following produce have been proposed for the following locations:

- Gherkins – Mahabubnagar, Rangareddy, Medak, Karimnagar, Warangal
- Mangoes and grapes – Hyderabad, Rangareddy, Medak, Mahabubnagar

Industries

The HITEC City is a major IT hub of Hyderabad

Several major manufacturing and services industries are in operation mainly around Hyderabad. Automobiles and auto components, spices, mines and minerals, textiles and apparels, pharmaceutical, horticulture, and poultry farming are the main industries in Telangana. In terms of services, Hyderabad is nicknamed "Cyberabad" due to the location of major software industries in the city. Prior to secession, it contributed 10% to India's and 98% to Andhra Pradesh's exports in the IT and ITES sectors in 2013 With Hyderabad in the front line of Telangana's goal to promote information technology in India, the city boasts the HITEC City as its premier hub.

The state government is in the process of developing industrial parks at different places, for specific groups of industries.

The existing parks are Software Park at Hyderabad, HITEC City for software units, Apparel Park at Gundlapochampalli, Export Promotion Park at Pashamylaram, Biotechnology park at Turkapally.

Hyderabad is also a major site for healthcare-related industries including hospitals and pharmaceutical organizations such as Nizam's Institute of Medical Sciences, Yashoda Hospitals, LV Prasad Eye Care, Akruti Institute of cosmetic and plastic surgery, Fever Hospital, Durgabai Deshmukh, Continental Hospitals and Apollo Hospitals.

Many pharmaceutical and pharmaceutical-related companies like Dr. Reddy's Laboratories, Shantha Biotechnics and GVK BIO are based out of Hyderabad.

In addition, Hyderabad-based healthcare non-profits include the Indian Heart Association, a cardiovascular disease NGO.

Tourism

Telangana State Tourism Development Corporation (TSTDC) is a state government agency which promotes tourism in Telangana. Telangana has a variety of tourist attractions including historical places, monuments, forts, waterfalls, forests and temples.

Awards

Telangana state has won CNBC-TV18's Promising State of the Year Award for the year of 2015. The Jury for the India Business Leader Awards (IBLA) has collectively chosen Telangana for the award.

INFRASTRUCTURE

Ramagundam Thermal Power station

Hyderabad Outer Ring Road

Secunderabad railway station

Power

Hydel and thermal power projects in the state meet the power requirements of the State. A number of new power projects are coming up in the State which is expected to generate additional power capacity in the state.

TRANSPORT

The state is well connected with other states by means of road, rail and airways. The Telangana State Road Transport Corporation (TSRTC) is the major public transport corporation that connects all the cities and villages. Mahatma Gandhi Bus Station (M.G.B.S) in Hyderabad is one of the largest bus stand in Asia. Jubilee Bus Station in Secunderabad serves inter city bus services.

Roadways

The state has a total of 16 national highways and accounts for a total length of 2,690.23 km (1,671.63 mi).

Railways

The history of railways in this region dates back to the time of Nizam of Hyderabad in 1874. It operates under the auspices of the South Central Railway founded in 1966. The landmark building Rail Nilayam in Secunderabad is the Zonal Headquarter office of South Central Railway. Secunderabad and Hyderabad are the main divisions of South Central Railway that fall in the state.

Airports

Rajiv Gandhi International Airport at Shamshabad is an international airport serving the city of Hyderabad It is the largest airport in the state and one of the busiest airports in the country. The government has plans to upgrade Warangal Airport, Nizamabad Airport and Ramagundam Airport It also plans to construct airports in Karimnagar and Kothagudem. Warangal has a domestic airport in Mamunooru which was established in the year 1930 during Nizam period. All the exports and imports of Azam Jahi Mills, Warangal were done through the Warangal Airport.

AGRICULTURE AND LIVESTOCK

Paddy fields in Warangal district

Rice is the major food crop and staple food of the state. Other important crops are tobacco, mango, cotton, and sugar cane. Agriculture has been the chief source of income for the state's economy. Important rivers of India, the Godavari, Krishna flow through the state, providing irrigation. Apart from major rivers, there are small rivers as Tunga Bhadra, Bima, Dindi, Kinnerasani, Manjeera, Manair, Penganga, Pranahitha, peddavagu and Taliperu. There are many multi-state irrigation projects in development, including Godavari River Basin Irrigation Projectsand Nagarjuna Sagar Dam, the world's highest masonry dam.

Given below is a table of 2015 national output share of select agricultural crops and allied segments in Telangana based on 2011 prices

Segment	National Share %
Ajwain	30.5
Cow pea	26.8

Chilli	16.0
Turmeric	13.7
Egg	12.4
Kapas	11.2
Fibre	10.5
Lemon	10.0
Bitter gourd	9.5
Meat	9.4
Tomato	8.9
Orange	8.7
Wool & hair	7.6
Maize	7.4
Mango	6.5
Cucumber	5.4
Bean	5.3

Agri Export Zones for the following produce are proposed at the places mentioned against them:

- Gherkins – Mahaboobnagar, Rangareddy, Medak, Karimnagar, Warangal
- Mangoes and Grapes - Hyderabad, Rangareddy, Medak, Mahaboobnagar

Telangana is developing into a seed hub in India, and was selects as a certifying agency as per OECD standards, for 10 states. The state cultivated seeds in 2,251 acres and exported 17,000 quintals to countries like Sudan, Egypt, Philippines and in 2017-18, it expanded cultivation to 2,567 acre and was expecting yield of 26,000 quintals.

Industries

Several major manufacturing and services industries are in operation mainly around Hyderabad. Automobiles and auto components industry, spices, mines and minerals, textiles and apparels, pharmaceutical, horticulture, poultry farming are the main industries in Telangana.

In terms of services, Hyderabad is usually nicknamed as Cyberabad due to its information technology foray and location of major software industries in the city. Prior to secession, it contributed 15% to India's and 98% to Andhra Pradesh's exports in IT and ITES sectors last 2013 With Hyderabad as in the front line of Telangana's aims to promote information technology in India, the city boasts the HITEC City as its premier hub.

The state government is in the process of developing Industrial Parks at different places, for specific groups of industries. The existing parks are Software Park at Hyderabad, HITEC City for software units, Apparel Park at Gundlapochampalli, Export Promotion Park at Pashamylaram, Bio-technology park at Turkapally.

Telangana, specifically Jubilee Hills, Hyderabad, is the headquarters of an international non-profit, the Indian Heart Association.

Services

Tourism

The Golconda Fort, Hyderabad

Telangana State Tourism Development Corporation

(TSTDC) is a state government agency which promotes tourism in Telangana. Telangana has a variety of tourist attractions including historical places, monuments, forts, water falls, forests and temples.

BUSINESS IN TELANGANA

Can I start business in Telangana?

While Hyderabad, the capital of Telangana, will continue to attract global investments for software and IT-related services, the government is concerned on the issue of industrialising its rural districts where much of its population exists.

To address the genuine worries of Telanganites, the government has passed a TS iPass Bill in the assembly that ensures self-certification and deemed approval of all clearances within three weeks of application for any mega project.

According to an estimate, the industrial policy with its novel TS iPass law for self-certification and time-bound approvals will attract not less than Rs 5 lakh crore investments in Hyderabad and its surrounding districts in the next decade.

Moreover, TRS government led by K. Chandrasekhar Rao has set up a single window clearance desk that enables speedy procedural sanctions for setting up industrial units or commercial ventures in Telangana.

Chasing cell to monitor approvals

The industrial policy is driven by the slogan of 'In Telangana - Innovate, Incubate, Incorporate' and has ushered in a regulatory system where doing business is made absolutely easy without any bureaucratic hassles.

Entrusted with the task of monitoring the approval of industrial projects, the chasing cell is expected to play a critical role in the setting up a whole range of factories, business centres and production units across the value chain of economic activity.

The right to clearance will involve a provision to impose a fine of Rs. 1,000 on officials for each day of delay in granting clearance to a project, besides allowing businesses to know the exact reason why a proposal is stuck.

The TS iPass law lays down a 15-day limit for the clearance of mega-projects involving over Rs. 200 crore and of one month for smaller projects.

But if the governments miss the clearance deadline, the project is said to have got automatic deemed approval and the promoters can ahead in setting up their plants (or enterprise).

Over 2 lakh acres land bank

A land bank of over 2 lakh acres have been set aside for industries even as several corporates have come forward to set up their plants in Telangana after it had unveiled its policy framework.

The government has taken up a thorough review of business rules and procedures to make administration efficient and people-centric.

And technology will be leveraged to the maximum in all its endeavours to realise the vision of the state leadership.

Chief Minister Chandrasekhar Rao has assured a 'corruption-free and trouble-free' system of governance without any room for lobbies, middlemen or extra-constitutional authorities which is indeed welcome sign for investors and corporate houses.

The policy framework intends to set up a regulatory mechanism where doing business would be as easy as shaking hands.

Super-fast broadband service

In a major initiative, the government has urged the internet giant Google to send a high-profile team to examine the possibility of Google Fibre, an optical fibre-based super-fast broadband services in the state.

Moreover, Google would set up a Greenfield facility, the largest outside the US and its first company-owned campus in Asia, at Gachibowli in Hyderabad.

It may be noted that Gachibowli is already home to global players such as Microsoft, Wipro, Infosys, Cap Gemini and Deloitte.

Spread over 7.2 acres, this 2-million sq ft facility will have the capacity for 14,000 employees once it becomes fully operations in 4-5 years time.

At present, Google operates from a rented facility at Kondapur in Hyderabad with 7,000 seats.

Once the super-fast broadband is laid underground, it will offer high-speed data connectivity and transmission which will further attract IT-related businesses in Hyderabad.

Amazon warehouse on city outskirts

In a boost to micro, small and medium industries, Amazon Seller Services has opened a fulfilment centre over an area of 2.80 lakh square feet on the outskirts of Hyderabad.

Similar to a warehouse depot, this Amazon fulfilment centre will ship a range of digital and electronic products from its inventory godowns to customers across the country who had made the purchases through the Amazon's e-commerce platform.

This warehouse near Hyderabad is the biggest investment by Amazon in India till date.

Amazon will be able to offer its services to thousands of small and medium business units in Telangana who will gain easy access to customers at a low operating cost.

According to Amazon company officials it is the easy of doing business in the state that has further prompted them to make investment and set up a fulfilment centre near Hyderabad.

This new facility of Amazon will do all the heavy lifting for small and medium scale units of the state and thus help them to grow profitability.

Training to SMEs on digital economy

Amazon Seller Services Pvt Ltd (ASSPL) has entered into an agreement with Telangana government to train thousands of small and medium enterprises on the e-commerce platforms and take advantage of the digital economy.

Under this pact, Amazon India will equip the SMEs through a series of seminars, workshops, video aids and ready reckoners on how to catalogue and manage the inventory for the e-commerce deals.

EMPLOYMENT LEVEL IN TELANGANA

The new government led by chief minister K. Chandrasekhar Rao has laid emphasis on rapid industrialisation to improve economic growth which will lead to higher employment opportunities for the youth.

According to 2011 census, the rural population of Telangana is 215.85 lakh representing 61.3% of the total population.

The high rural population has made their economic development and livelihood issues as critical factors for the overall progress of the state.

Hence, the rural development department is actively monitoring the implementation of schemes like watershed development, SHGs welfare programmes and Mahatma Gandhi National Rural Employment Guarantee Scheme (MGNREGS) at the grassroots level.

Telangana Academy for Skill and Knowledge (TASK)

In order to address the growing unemployment in the state, TASK has been set up to provide training to graduates and make them ready to meet the needs of the various industries.

The training module at TASK has been designed to produce enough number of readily employable graduates through skill induction.

In fact, this centre has been training both the engineering and degree students in communication skills, employability attitude and technical skills with the deployment of experienced mentors from various partnering colleges.

Apart from entering into broad-based agreements with MNCs, the academy is working closely with giant corporations like IBM, Oracle, Infosys, TCS, Tech Mahindra, Autodesk, Google, Cognizant and HCL, among others with the main aim to extend gainful employment to Telangana youths.

Over 12 lakh Telangana youths jobless

Telangana government is making efforts to set up its own State Public Service commission, even as the unemployment is growing rapidly ever since the launch of statehood movement.

After formation of Telangana state, unemployed graduates are eagerly awaiting the recruitment notifications of government jobs including the setting up of the first state PSC.

During statehood stir, the Andhra Pradesh Public Service Commission has delayed in issuing the notifications for government jobs leading much heartburn among the aspirants.

At present, Telangana has over 12 lakh unemployed youths across its 10 districts, according to informal sources.

Given the severity of the problem, Telangana government is keen to set up the State Public Service Commission at the earliest and issue notification for the conduct of exams for filling up of existing vacancies across departments.

More importantly, the government has to prepare an academic calendar for filling up job vacancies and select an agency that can issue notifications and take care of related academic matters without giving any scope for corruption.

Recruitment to fill 25,000 vacant posts

Notwithstanding the ongoing process of allocation to government employees, steps are on to fill the backlog of 25,000 vacant posts in departments.

The process of regularising the services of all contract employees would also be taken up in phased manner to be completed by the end of 2015.

While obstacles are being faced in the allocation of employees, it has been decided to fill up 25,000 vacant posts at the same time and the notifications will be issued in due course.

TRS chief and CM K. Chandrasekhar Rao has assured one lakh government jobs in the next two years (2015-16 and 2016-17) through Telangana Public Service Commission (TSPCS) which will issue notifications for the exams.

Great response to Varadhi Society

Several hundreds of unemployed youths had registered with the Varadhi Society to get employment in the government and private sector.

Varadhi society is a registered body with district collector as its chairman and other members include DRDA project director, district employment officer and its secretary is a retired deputy collector.

The Varadhi will send SMS alerts on the employment opportunities and hold training programmes for various competitive examinations.

Varadhi Society will also conduct pre-recruitment training programmes in various skills and trades to provide employment across industry verticals.

Growing campus unrest

The graduates and unemployed youths are running out of patients as the new government is yet to come out with notifications for filling up thousands of government jobs.

While the main reason for Telangana stir is that the statehood will open up more job opportunities for youth of this region as earlier a major chunk of plum postings and government jobs were taken away by people from Seemandhra region, nothing seems to work in the favour of Telanganities even after the formation of new state.

Industrialisation holds the key for achieving higher growth trajectory and employment generation. Realising this, the new Government has laid adequate emphasis on rapid industrialisation in the State.

The State is already the favoured destination for many investors from India and abroad due to its natural resources, availability of skilled manpower and technological base. In order to capitalise on these advantages, the new leadership is taking several steps to improve the investment climate in the State.

INDUSTRIAL SCENARIO OF TELANGANA

At the core of the new industrial policy unveiled in June 2015 by Chief Minister K. Chandrasekhar Rao to a large gathering of top corporates and business houses in Hyderabad is the time-bound, speedy clearance to investment projects.

TS-iPASS features

The key feature of this new policy is its quick approval process through a self-certification mechanism.

Called Telangana State - Industrial Project Approval and Self Certification System, this process will help an entrepreneur start his or her business smoothly without hurdles and at the same time apply for official clearances.

The policy prescribes norms for giving permissions to mega projects with investments of Rs 200 crore and above; large consisting of Rs 10 crore-Rs 200 crore; and small and medium project proposals. The clearances would be given in two weeks and in case, one can't get this done, the project is deemed to have been approved by the government.

If any official is found causing unnecessary delay in project approvals, then a fine of Rs 1,000 per day would be imposed on him or her.

The iPASS would have state-level and district-level committees to ensure smooth flow in the processing the applications and according permission.

Notable points

1. Online system for filling and issue of clearances.
2. A single application form that lists the requirements from different government departments.

3. Self-certification
4. Project deemed approved if permission is not given within a timeframe.
5. Right to get clearances.
6. Penal actions against officials if failed to give permissions in time.

Six industrial corridors

Telangana will develop six industrial corridors along national and state highways. On a fast track basis, the government will be developing Hyderabad-Warangal, Hyderabad-Nagpur and Hyderabad-Bengaluru sectors.

In the second phase, industrial corridors will be developed along state highways from Hyderabad to Macherial, Nalgonda and Khammam.

On a priority basis, the Hyderabad-Warangal corridor will be set up in the fiscal 2015-16.

The state will add 3,000 MW of electricity in 2015-16 to the existing capacity of 4,300 MW to address power shortage. And has drawn up plans to add another 24,000 MW by 2018.

BHEL was developing 6,000 MW projects in Telangana and by the end of 2015-16, it will add 1,700 MW while another 1,000 MW will be commissioned next year.

The state aims to commission at least 5,000 MW of solar power in the next four years.

It is proposed to use 10% of water under Telangana water grid for industrial purposes and an outlay of Rs 30,000 crore will be spent to ensure availability of drinking water to every household in the state.

Telangana has set aside 1.5 lakh acres of land for setting up new industrial units which will have plug-n-play facilities.

Pharma city and university

A pharma city and a pharma university would be developed to give further impetus to this sector as the state accounts for one-third of pharma industry in the country. Moreover, the government would take up the burden of treating the effluents from the pharma units.

Already, 11,000 acres of land has been identified for the pharma city at Mucherla in Ranga Reddy district near Hyderabad.

While Hyderabad is reputed for its software exports, the government is making all out efforts to diversify the industrial basket.

The government identified 14 core areas for a focused approach including life sciences, pharma, IT, aerospace, automobiles, textiles, minerals, and transportation and logistics.

Food processing, plastic and polymers, FMCG, engineering and capital goods, gems and jewellery, waste management, renewable energy, and wood-based industries are the other thrust areas.

The manufacturing accounted for for 27.9% of the GDP against the national average of 17% and Telangana is among the top three states in the country in terms of contribution of factories to the GDP is concerned.

The policy offers special incentives for entrepreneurs belonging to women, SC and STs and mandates the TS Industrial Infrastructure Corporation (TSIIC) to get statutory clearances for the industrial parks.

As part of an industrial eco-system there are plans to created industrial townships at select locations so that people could reside there and commute to work without any hassles.

ITC to invest Rs 8,000 crore in Telangana

Welcoming the steps to ensure speedy clearances, ITC chairman Y.C. Deveshwar has said his company will invest Rs 8,000 crore to expand its paper-making capacity in the state, setting up a food processing unit and a couple of hotels.

The investment into paperboard alone would take about Rs 4,500 crore which would double the capacity at its Badrachalam plant in Khammam district from 5 lakh tonnes to one million tonnes per annum.

INFRASTRUCTURE OF TELANGANA

A fast growing state like Telangana is in urgent need of infrastructure upgrades like well-connected roads, railways and airports, besides round-the-clock power supply and irrigation channels for robust growth of industry as well as agriculture.

Energy supply in Telangana

Being a power intensive state with a per capita power consumption of 985 units against the national average of 917 units (2012-13), the state is drawing up frenetic plans to augment its production capacity through progressive steps across the value chain of fuel-generation-transmission-distribution cycle to meet the various needs of industries and consumers.

However, the state has to contend with growing power deficit which is expected to touch 40,472 MU (million units) in 2018-19 with requirement at 84,496 MU as against the supply from existing sources at only 43,754 MU.

The urban development in Hyderabad and phased urbanisation in other towns of Nizamabad, Karimnagar and Warangal would need exponential power in the coming years.

Moreover, some of the big ticket projects such as metro rail, Hyderabad IT Investment Region (ITIR), Hyderabad-Nagpur industrial corridor and lift irrigation schemes would boost the demand for steady power.

Solar energy

The estimated solar potential in Telangana is 20.41 GW and the government is keen to promote renewable power in the state with emphasis on solar plants at select locations.

The solar roof top net metering system is being encouraged to reduce the pressure on grid supply with subsidy from the Centre. It was decided to extend 30% subsidy in the domestic sector for 1 KW of grid system for 4,200 numbers in addition to the Centre's subsidy.

Road network

The roads and buildings department is maintaining a total road network of 26,837 km in the state.

The widening of single lane roads to double lane roads is being taken up for improving the connectivity between the different mandal and district headquarters. Under this scheme, 143 works covering 149 mandals for a distance of 1,996 kms at a cost of Rs 2,585.00 crore have been taken up.

A number of important single lane roads are being made into double lane roads with an aim to improve the connectivity for the entire state.

Under this scheme, 260 works for a length of 2,721 kms at an estimated cost of Rs 3,704 crore have been taken up.

Hyderabad airport

Hyderabad International Airport Ltd owns and operates the Rajiv Gandhi International Airport (RGIA).

This is a PPP project and the total investment for the airport construction in the first phase is Rs 2,920 crore.

RGHIAL is a joint venture company promoted by GMR Group (63%) with Malaysia Airports Holding Berhad (MAHB) (11%), state government (13%) and the AAI (13%) as the other consortium partners.

During 2014-15 (April 14 - December 14), domestic passenger growth is around 20% year on year (YoY), whereas international passenger growth is 13%.

Overall the passenger traffic has shown a growth of 18% YoY. In the same period the airport handled 7.75 million passengers.

For 2014-15 (April 14 – December 14) the growth of domestic cargo is around 18% YoY, while international cargo volume has grown by 13%.

The overall the cargo has shown a growth of 15% YoY. In the same period, the airport handled 77,266 tonnes of cargo.

Irrigation

The utilisation of water from Godavari and Krishna rivers, tributaries, tanks and ponds have been the major source of irrigation in Telangana.

In all, there are about 46,000 water conservation structures from very large tanks to small ponds including percolation tanks. These structures are the leading sources for meeting the irrigation of both commercial and domestic needs.

A grand strategy has been designed to facilities for irrigating one lakh acres in each assembly constituency of Telangana excluding urban areas in the coming 5 years.

Thus the government has proposed to take up two major projects and one flood flow canal that would benefit the districts of Mahabubnagar, Ranga Reddy, Nalgonda and Warangal by irrigating 13.41 lakh acres and check the floods in the monsoon season.

There are 35,974 tanks serving an ayacut of 18.75 lakh acres including 31,196 panchayat tanks serving an ayacut of 6.68 lakh acres.

The rehabilitation of minor irrigation schemes sanctioned under a World Bank assisted Telangana Community Based Tank Management Project is in progress and would improve 1,182 tanks and nearly 762 schemes were completed so far.

Mission Kakatiya

Telangana has taken up a massive programme of restoring all the 46,531 minor irrigation sources under the project Mission Kakatiya in a decentralised manner through community involvement.

The government is aiming to complete the restoration of all the tanks in the next five years from 2015 at an estimated cost of Rs 20,000 crore.

Infrastructure support

Some of the features that have become a part of larger policies in order to create an eco-system for speedy industrialisation of the state:

1. Provision of Rs 100 crore in budget every year for the promotion of roads, power, water and waste management under the Industrial Infrastructure Development Fund (IIDF) Scheme.
2. Promotion of National Manufacturing Investment Zone (NMIZ) along national highways to capitalise on the strengths in line with the Centre's initiatives for value addition within the state.
3. Promotion of industrial corridors for the optimum utilisation of resources.
4. Reservation of 30-40% of the land for MSMEs in the industrial estates developed by Telangana Industrial Infrastructure Corporation (TSIIC).
5. Allocation of 15.44% of plots to SC entrepreneurs and 9.34% of plots to ST entrepreneurs in the new industrial estates and preferential allotment to SC,ST entrepreneurs in the existing estates.
6. Allocation of 10% of plots to women entrepreneurs in the new industrial estates

SOFTWARE INDUSTRY IN TELANGANA

The Indian state of Telangana has a significant amount of software export in India. While the majority of the industry is concentrated in Hyderabad, other cities are also becoming significant IT destinations in the state.

Chandrababu Naidu, current Andhra Pradesh Chief Minister is the visionary behind the development software industry in Telangana. In Hyderabad, the central region of the business happens in HITEC City, in the Madhapur suburb. Development of HITEC City prompted several IT and ITES companies to set up operations in the city, and has led civic boosters to call their city "Cyberabad." There have been extensive investments in digital infrastructure in Telangana.

Cyber Towers, HITEC City, Hyderabad.

The IT exports exports from Hyderabad stood second in the country at 93,442 crore in FY 2017-18 improving from previous year 85,470 crore ($13 billion, 14% CAGR) in FY 2016-17 The target is to increase it to 1.2 lac crore by 2020.

Telangana ICT policy

The initiation of this Software Industry in Hyderabad was done in parallel to other major cities in India in the early 1990's. Present Chief Minister, K. Chandrasekhar Rao(KCR) created the Telangana IT policy 2016.

Notable people

- Srini Raju Co-Founder and Chairman of Peepul Capital (successor to iLabs Venture Capital Fund), a Private Equity (PE) firm based out of Hyderabad and Chennai.

7

Tourism

TOURISM IN TELANGANA

Telangana State Tourism Development Corporation (TSTDC) is a state government agency which promotes tourism in Telangana, a state in the Southern region of India. Retired Director General of Police Pervaram Ramulu appointed as First chairman of Telangana State Tourism. Tourist attractions in Telangana include historical places, monuments, forts, water falls, forests and temples.

Hyderabad, the state capital, ranked second best place in the world that one should see in 2015 which is published in the annual guide of 'Traveler' magazine of National Geographic.

In order to reinvent Telangana as an important socio-cultural landscape, tourism is given much emphasis for it has the potential to expose the cultural heritage and ecological sites to visitors from within and outside the state in addition to earning revenues and creating jobs.

All the cultural, religious and natural sites are given a facelift to promote tourism. The capital outlays for infrastructure growth in tourist spots and circuits are being set aside.

The scenic Hussain Sagar Lake in Hyderabad is cleaned up under an ambitious project aimed to improve the environs and safeguard this precious water body from misuse. Once investment is channelised for the lake clean up, it will boost the tourist arrivals to this popular spot in the city.

In order to promote the cultural heritage, Yadagirigutta, a holy place near Hyderabad and much revered in this state, is developed as a global religious centre and funds were allocated for the celebration of 'Godavari Pushkaralu' with the usual pomp and grandeur.

Showcasing Hyderabad

This high tech city was ranked the second among the "Best of the World - 20 Places You Should see in 2015" list, published in the annual guide of National Geographic Traveller magazine.

The heritage sites in Hyderabad offer cultural diversity and tailor-made tour packages take visitors - both domestic and foreign travellers - to places in and around Hyderabad.

Telangana State Tourism Development Corporation (TSTDC) has a Nizam palaces package covering Falaknuma and Chowmahalla palaces, a Hyderabad by night daily tour that includes a sound and light show at Golconda Fort and Taramati Baradari, a historical sarai (caravan inn) as part of Ibrahim Bagh, a Persian style garden built during the reign of Ibrahim Quli Qutub Shah, the second Sultan of Golconda.

Qutub Shahi tombs are being conserved with the Centre's assistance, even as Aga Khan Trust is collaborating with the government in a big project to restore and beautify tombs.

Funds for tourist infrastructure

Suitable packages and developing amenities to attract tourists to lesser known destinations spread across the districts have been taken up the government with necessary funding.

Niti Aayog of the Centre has sanctioned a grant of Rs 33 crore to develop infrastructure at Nagarjuna Sagar, Karimnagar, Ramappa, Kinnerasani, Kothagudem and Gajwel.

Exclusive district plans for the development of tourism spots in all the 10 districts of Telangana are being drafted and expected to be approved shortly.

Telangana is gifted with a number of beautiful temples and ancient places of worship that have turned out to be busy pilgrim centres attracting millions of devotees throughout the year.

One such circuit started by TSTDC covers Chilkur Balaji temple on the banks of Osman Sagar Lake near Hyderabad.

Telangana Tourism is offering similar packages to visit Sitaramachandra Swamy temple at Bhadrachalam (Khammam), Saraswati temple at Basara (Adilabad) and Laxmi Narasimha Swamy Temple at Yadagirigutta (Nalgonda).

A number of amenities for tourists are put in place at Vemulawada Sri Raja Rajeshwara Swamy temple , Hanuman temple at Kondagattu and Narasimha Swamy temple at Dharmapuri in Karimnagar district, Ramappa temple at Palampet in Warangal district and Jogulamba temple at Alampur in Mahabubnagar district.

Rural Tourism of Telangana

As Telangana is rich in rural handicrafts and customs, the union ministry at the Centre has identified a number of tourism projects in consonance with the living traditions of the region - Pochampally (Nalgonda), Nirmal (Adilabad), Cheriyal and Pembarthi (Warangal) - all of which have their unique art of fabric weaving being passed on to generations through the force of habit.

Handicrafts, perhaps, represent the oldest living culture of Telanganites who still depend on these ancient vocations for their livelihood.

Wildlife and Eco Tourism

Blessed with forests and wildlife sanctuaries, the state offers much scope for wildlife tourism for nature lovers.

Some of the most visited places are: Alisagar Deer park in Nizamabad; Eturunagaram sanctuary and Pakhal wildlife sanctuary in Warangal; Kawal wildlife sanctuary in Jannaram; Pranahitha wildlife sanctuary and Sivaram wildlife sanctuary in

Adilabad; Mahavir Harina Vanasthali National Park, Vansthalipuram; Nehru Zoological park in Hyderabad; Manjira Bird Sanctuary in Sangareddy; Pocharam sanctuary in Medak and Shamirpet deer park in Rangareddy.

Heritage Tourism of Telangana

A land dotted with forts, heritage sites and monuments, Telangana is developing amenities and other facilities at a number of places to facilitate tourist flow.

Tourism department has undertaken projects at forts in Golconda, Medak, Khammam, Nizamabad, Elagandula (Karimnagar) and Bhongir (Nalgonda).

It is to be noted that Warangal and Golconda forts host a sound and light show that recreate the magnificent past of bygone eras for the benefit of tourists.

TSTDC has proposed to uplift a number of heritage sites with sound and light shows which will amplify the rich historical moorings of these places. Moreover, travel packages are being organised that also connect to neighbouring states.

As part of tourism promotion, TSTDC runs Harita hotel chains, roadside amenities, river cruises and majestic waterfalls at scenic locations.

However, a visit to Telangana is never complete without tasting its cuisine, notably Hyderabadi Biryani, Qubani-ka-Meetha, Haleem, and Irani Chai.

Medical Tourism of Telangana

A range of world-class healthcare treatments at affordable prices are being offered at elite hospitals in Hyderabad which get a steady stream of foreign patients for availing medical services.

With a huge untapped potential to emerge as global hub for medical tourism, steps are being finalised to prepare a comprehensive policy for this sub-sector and road shows will also be conducted to woo foreign patients to Telangana.

Bathukamma of Telangana

An annual floral festival enjoying state patronage, Bathukamma gets tourists from all over the country to appreciate the cultural heritage of Telanganites.

The government has released Rs 10 crore for conduct of this festival in 2014 and has plans to conduct Bathukamma on a grand scale each year.

On the eve of this floral event, tour packages are organised by TSTDC to facilitate visitors eager to witness floral decorations and cultural events associated with Bathukamma.

Bonalu in Telangana

Telangana tourism is planning to organise Bonalu weekend package tours to Ujjaini Mahankali temple in Secunderabad and Maisamma temple at Lal Darwaza.

The tableau of Telangana state which was displayed for the first time at Rajpath in New Delhi during the Republic Day 2014 parade depicted Bonalu festival in a colorful manner.

Sammakka Saralamma Jatara

Also known as Medaram Jatara, this festival is celebrated in a remote area of Warangal district. It is said that after Kumbha Mela, the Medaram Jatara attracts the largest number of devotees in the country.

More than one crore devotees visited Medaram during the Jatara in 2014. This festival is celebrated once in every two years at the same location with one of the largest gatherings of devotees.

KUNTALA WATERFALL

Kuntala Waterfall is waterfall located in Kuntala, Adilabad district, Telangana. It is located on Kadem river in Neredigonda mandal. It is the highest waterfall in the state of Telangana, with a height of 147 feet (45 meters).

These waterfalls are in the dense forests inhabited by the Gonds. Kunta in Gondi and Telugu language means pond.

Kuntalu means several ponds. The waterfall originates from a confluence of several ponds that lead to the river.

Formed by the Kadam River, Kuntala falls cascades down through two steps and can be seen as two separate adjacent falls after the peak rains. It is one of the famous one day outings from Hyderabad. There is a motorable road until the entry point of the falls, from where steps are available to reach the bottom of the falls. The falls is about 10 minutes (one way) walk from the entry point.

Transportation

Public transport is available until Neredikonda, from where private vehicles can be hired. Nirmal and Adilabad are base stations. Other waterfalls in the area include Gayatri Waterfalls and Pochera Falls.

The nearest airport is Rajiv Gandhi International Airport in Hyderabad (310 km).

The nearest railway station is Adilabad Railway Station (58 km).

CHARMINAR

The Charminar ("Four Minarets"), constructed in 1591, is a monument and mosque located in Hyderabad, Telangana, India. The landmark has become a global icon of Hyderabad, listed among the most recognized structures of India. Charminar has been a historical place with Mosque on the top floor for over 400 years and also known for its surrounding markets. It is one of the tourist attractions in Hyderabad. It is where many local festivals are celebrated, such as Ramzaan.

The Charminar is situated on the east bank of Musi river. To the west lies the Laad Bazaar, and to the southwest lies the richly ornamented granite Makkah Masjid. It is listed as an archaeological and architectural treasure on the official "List of Monuments" prepared by the Archaeological Survey of India. The English name is a translation and combination of the Urdu words *Châr* and *Minar* or *meenar*, translating to "Four Pillars";

the eponymous towers are ornate minarets attached and supported by four grand arches.

History

The fifth ruler of the Qutb Shahi dynasty, Muhammad Quli Qutb Shah, built the Charminar in 1591 after shifting his capital from Golkondato the newly formed city of Hyderabad.

Charminar, Char Kaman and Gulzar Houz, photographed by Lala Deen Dayal in the 1880s

The Archaeological Survey of India (ASI), the current caretaker of the structure, mentions in its records, "There are various theories regarding the purpose for which Charminar was constructed. However, it is widely accepted that Charminar was built at the center of the city, to commemorate the eradication of Cholera", a deadly disease which was wide spread at that time. Muhammad Quli Qutb Shah had prayed for the end of the plague that was ravaging his city and vowed to build a Mosque at the very place where he prayed. According to Jean de Thévenot, a French traveller of the 17th century whose narration was complemented with the available Persian texts, the Charminar was constructed in the year 1591 CE, to commemorate the beginning of the second Islamic millennium year (1000 AH). The event was celebrated far and wide in the Islamic world, thus Qutb Shah founded the city of Hyderabad to celebrate the event and commemorate it with the construction of this building.Due to its architecture it is also called as Arc de Triomphe of the east.

The Charminar was constructed at the intersection of the historical trade route that connects the markets of Golkonda with the port city of Machilipatnam. The Old City of Hyderabad was designed with Charminar as its centerpiece. The city was spread around the Charminar in four different quadrants and chambers, segregated according to the established settlements. Towards the north of Charminar is the Char Kaman, or four gateways, constructed in the cardinal direction. Additional eminent architects from Persia were also invited to develop the city plan. The structure itself was intended to serve as a Mosque and Madarsa. It is of Indo-Islamic architecture style, incorporating Persian architectural elements.

Historian Masud Hussain Khan says that the construction of Charminar was completed in the year 1592, and that it is the city of Hyderabad which was actually founded in the year 1591. According to the book "Days of the Beloved", Qutb shah constructed the Charminar in the year 1589, on the very spot where he first glimpsed his future queen Bhagmati, and after her conversion to Islam, Qutb Shah renamed the city as "Hyderabad". Though the story was rejected by the historians and scholars, it became popular folklore among the locals.

Qutb Shah was also among the early poets of Dakhani Urdu. While laying the foundation of Charminar, he performed the prayers in Dakhini couplets, which are recorded as follows:

Fill this city of mine with people as,

You filled the river with fishes *O Lord.*

During the Mughal governorship between Qutb Shahi and Asaf Jahi rule, the southwestern minaret "fell to pieces" after being struck by lightning and was repaired at a cost of Rs.60,000. In 1824, the monument was replastered at a cost of Rs. One lakh.

Structure

The Charminar masjid is a square structure with each side 20 meters (approximately 66 feet) long, with four grand arches each facing a fundamental point that open into four streets. At each corner stands an exquisitely shaped minaret, 56 meters (approximately 184 feet) high, with a double balcony. Each minaret is crowned by a bulbous dome with dainty petal-like designs at the base. Unlike the minarets of Taj Mahal, Charminar's four fluted minarets are built into the main structure. There are 149 winding steps to reach the upper floor. The structure is also known for its profusion of stucco decorations and the arrangement of its balustrades and balconies.

The structure is made of granite, limestone, mortar and pulverized marble and it weighs approximately 14000 tones. Initially the monument with its four arches was so proportionately planned that when the fort was opened one could catch a glimpse of the bustling Hyderabad city, as these Charminar arches were facing the most active royal ancestral streets.

There is also a legend of an underground tunnel connecting the Golconda fort to Charminar, possibly intended as an escape route for the Qutb Shahi rulers in case of a siege, though the location of the tunnel is unknown.

A mosque is located at the western end of the open roof; remaining part of the roof served as a court during the Qutb Shahi times. The actual mosque occupies the top floor of the four-storey structure. A vault which appears from inside like a dome supports two galleries within the Charminar, one over another, and above those a terrace that serves as a roof, bordered with a stone balcony. The main gallery has 45 covered prayer spaces with a large open space in front to accommodate more people for Friday prayers.

The clock on the four cardinal directions was added in 1889.

There is a vazu (water cistern) in the middle, with a small fountain for ablution before offering prayer in the Charminar mosque.

Surrounding Area

The area surrounding Charminar is also known by the same name. It falls under the Charminar constituency.

Makkah Masjid

The monument overlooks another grand mosque called the Makkah Masjid. Muhammad Quli Qutb Shah, the 5th ruler of the Qutb Shahi dynasty, commissioned bricks to be made from the soil brought from Mecca, the holiest site of Islam, and used them in the construction of the central arch of the mosque, hence its name.

Bazaars

Char Kaman seen from the top of the Charminar.

A market exists around Charminar. Lad Bazaar is known for its jewelry, especially bangles, and the Pathar Gatti, which is known for its pearls. In its heyday, the Charminar market had some 14,000 shops. The Bazaars surrounding Charminar were described in the poem "In the Bazaars of Hyderabad" by Sarojini Naidu.

Char Kaman and Gulzar Houz

Four arches to the North of Charminar are known as Char Kaman. These were built along with the Charminar in the 16th century. These are the *Kali Kaman*, *Machli Kaman*, *Seher-e-Batil ki Kaman* and *Charminar Kaman*. At the center of these arches is a fountain called the Gulzar Houz. The Char Kaman are in dire need of restoration, and protection from encroachments.

Influences

In 2007, Hyderabadi Muslims living in Pakistan constructed a small-scaled quasi replica of the Charminar at the main crossing of the Bahadurabad neighborhood in Karachi.

Lindt chocolatier Adelbert Boucher created a scaled model of the Charminar out of 50 kilograms of chocolate. The model, which required three days' labour, was on display at The Westin, Hyderabad, India on 25 and 26 September 2010.

The Charminar Express is an express train named after the Charminar, which runs between Hyderabad and Chennai.

The Charminar also appears on coins and banknotes of the defunct Hyderabadi Rupee, the currency of the erstwhile Hyderabad State.

As an icon of the city of Hyderabad as well as the Telangana State, the structure also appears on the Emblem of Telangana, along with the Kakatiya Kala Thoranam.

Pedestrianization Project

The "Charminar Pedestrianization Project" was instituted by the then combined Government of Andhra Pradesh in partnership with the Greater Hyderabad Municipal Corporation. The project was initiated in 2006 with an investment of Rs 35 crore. Out of Rs.35 crore, the share of Central government funds stood at Rs 12.28 crore while the State government gave Rs 5.26 crore. However, the project did not see the light of day due to various factors such as Telangana movement, illegal encroachments by hawkers, vehicular traffic, and illegal street vendors. Later during January 2017, the new Government of Telangana introduced a 14-member French Delegation to takeover the project to assess the feasibility in developing the monument as an eco-friendly tourism and heritage destination. The team has inspected surrounding areas such as the Gulzar house, Macca Masjid, Lad Bazar, and Sardar Mahal. Subsequently, the project took over on a brisk pace and is expected to be completed by May 2018.

UNESCO World Heritage Site-Tentative List

Charminar, along with the Qutb Shahi Monuments of Hyderabad: the Golconda Fort, and the Qutb Shahi Tombs, were included in the "tentative list" of UNESCO World Heritage Site. The Monument was submitted by the Permanent Delegation of India to UNESCO on September 10, 2010.

Temple Structure

A Hindu temple named Bhagyalakshmi Temple is located at the base of Charminar. A Hindu trust manages the temple dedicated to the Goddess Lakshmi. The Archaeological Survey of India (ASI) which manages the Charminar has declared the temple structure as an unauthorised construction. Hyderabad High Court has stopped any further expansion of the temple. While the origin of the temple is currently disputed, the current structure that houses the idol was erected in the 1960s. In 2012, *The Hindu* newspaper published an old photograph showing that the temple structure never existed. The Hindu also released a note asserting the authenticity of the photographs, and clearly stated that there was no temple structure in photos taken in 1957 and 1962. Additionally, it showed photos that provide evidence that the temple is a recent structure - a temple structure can be seen in photos taken in 1990 and 1994. Also, a temple is seen in a photograph taken in

1986 which is kept in the Aga Khan Visual Archive, MIT Libraries' collections, United States, but not in the earlier ones.

QUTB SHAHI TOMBS

The Qutb Shahi Tombs are located in the Ibrahim Bagh (garden precinct), close to the famous Golconda Fort in Hyderabad, India. They contain the tombs and mosques built by the various kings of the Qutb Shahi dynasty. The galleries of the smaller tombs are of a single storey while the larger ones are two storied. In the centre of each tomb is a sarcophagus which overlies the actual burial vault in a crypt below. The domes were originally overlaid with blue and green tiles, of which only a few pieces now remain.

Location

They lie in the north of the outer perimeter wall of Golkonda Fort and its BanjarI Darwaza (Gate of the Gipsies, or itinerant merchants), amidst the Ibrahim Bagh.

Description

The tombs form a large cluster and stand on a raised platform. The tombs are domed structures built on a square base surrounded by pointed arches, a distinctive style that blends Persian, Pashtun and Hindu forms. The tombs are structures with intricately carved stonework and are surrounded by landscaped gardens.

The tombs were once furnished with carpets, chandeliers and velvet canopies on silver poles. Copies of the *Quran* were kept on pedestals and readers recited verses from the holy book at regular intervals. Golden spires were fitted over the tombs of the sultans to distinguish their tombs from those of other members of the royal family.

History

During the Qutb Shahi period, these tombs were held in great veneration. But after their reign, the tombs were neglected until Sir Salar Jung III ordered their restoration in the early

19th century. A garden was laid out, and a compound wall was built. Once again, the tomb-garden of the Qutb Shahi family became a place of serene beauty. All except the last of the Qutb Shahi sultans lie buried here.

Sultan Quli Qutb Mulk's tomb, the style of which sets the example for the tombs of his descendants, is on an elevated terrace measuring 30 meters in each direction. The tomb chamber proper is octagonal, with each side measuring around 10 meters. The entire structure is crowned by a circular dome. There are three graves in this tomb chamber and twenty-one laid out on the surrounding terrace, all of which lack inscription except for the main tomb. The inscription on Sultan Quli's tomb is in three bands, in the Naskh and Tauq scripts. The inscription refers to Sultan Quli as *Bade Malik* (Great Master) — the endearing term by which all people of the Deccan used for him. The tomb was built in 1543 A.D. by the Sultan, during his lifetime, as was the custom.

Near the tomb of Sultan Quli is that of his son, Jamsheed, the second in the line of Qutb Shahi sultans. Built in 1550 A.D., this is the only Qutb Shahi tomb which has not been fashioned from shining black basalt. Its appearance, too, is quite unlike the other tombs in the garden — it rises gracefully in two stories, unlike the squat tombs of the other kings. Jamsheed Quli Qutb Shah's is the only tomb of a Qutb Shahi ruler without any inscriptions; of course, Jamsheed's son, Subhan's tomb also does not have any inscriptions. Subhan Quli Qutb Shah ruled for a short time. Subhan's tomb stands midway between the tombs of his father and grandfather. He was popularly called *Chhote Malik* (Small Master).

Sultan Ibrahim Quli Qutb Shah's tomb, built in 1580, after his death, is slightly larger than Sultan Quli's tomb. Traces of the enameled tiles, which once adorned this mausoleum, can still be seen on the southern wall. The tomb has two graves in the main chamber and 16 on the terrace; some of them probably are those of his six sons and three daughters. There are inscriptions in the Thuluth script on all faces of the sarcophagus. The three famous calligraphists — Isphalan, Ismail and Taqiuddin Muhammad Salih — who left a store of Naskh, Thuluth and Nastaliq inscriptions on the many Qutb Shahi edifices in the city, were contemporaries of Ibrahim Shah.

The Great Mosque in the Qutb Shahi Tombs Complex

Sultan Muhammed Quli Qutb Shah's mausoleum is considered the grandest of the Qutb Shahi tombs. Built in 1602 A.D., the tomb is on a terrace of 65m square and 4m high. A flight of steps leads to the mausoleum proper, which is 22 m square on the outside and 11 m square on the inside. There are entrances on the southern and eastern sides. The tomb is in a vault below the terrace. Inscriptions in Persian and the Naskh scripts decorate it.

Another grand mausoleum is that of the sixth sultan, Muhammed Qutb Shah. The facade of this tomb was once decorated with enameled tiles; only traces are now evident. There are six graves and inscriptions in Thuluth and Naskh. The mausoleum was built in 1626. Sultan Abdullah Qutb Shah's tomb is the last of the royal tombs, as Abul Hasan Qutb Shah(Tana Shah), the last Qutb Shahi Sultan, was a prisoner in the fortress of Daulatabad, near Aurangabad, when he died. While the tombs of those who ruled dominate the area, interspersed are many other monuments, most of them tombs of other members of the royal family.

The tomb of Fatima Sultan, with its bulbous dome, is near the entrance to the tomb-garden. Fatima was the sister of Muhammed Qutb Shah. Her tomb houses several graves, two with inscriptions.

Immediately to the south of Muhammed Quli's tomb are three uninscribed tombs. There are the mausoleums of Kulthoom, Muhammed Qutb Shahi's granddaughter born of the son of the sultan's favourite wife Khurshid Bibi, her (Kulthoom's) husband and daughter. Kulthoom's tomb is on the west of this cluster.

The twin-tombs of the two favourite *hakims* (physicians) of Sultan Abdullah — Nizamuddin Ahmed Gilani and Abdul Jabbar Gilani — were built in 1651. They are among the few Qutb Shahi tombs that are not of royalty. Another pair are those of Premamati and Taramati, the favourite courtesans of Sultan Abdullah Shah, were laid to rest beside his tomb. One other tomb which is not that of a Qutb Shahi family member is that of Neknam Khan. Neknam Khan, who served in Abdullah's army, was the commander-in-chief of the Carnatic. His tomb is on a platform outside the mausoleum of Ibrahim Qutb Shah. It was built in 1672, two years after Nekam Khan's death.

The last Sultan of the dynasty, Abul Hasan Qutb Shah (also known as *Tana Shah*) was not buried alongside his ancestor. Instead, he was buried at Khuldabad. The mausoleum which Abul Hasan, the last Qutb Shahi Sultan, began building for himself, actually houses the grave of Mir Ahmed, the son of Sultan Abdullah's son-in-law and the sister of Abbas II Safair, the Shah of Persia. The tomb of Fadma Khanum, one of Sultan Abdullah's daughters, stands near the mausoleum of her husband, Mir Ahmed. Hers is the only Qutb Shahi tomb not surmounted by a dome.

To the west of the tombs lies the dargah of Hussain Shah Wali, the revered Sufi saint. He is most affectionately remembered by people as the builder of Hussain Sagar in 1562. Among other monuments in the garden that are not tombs, the most important are the mortuary bath and the Masjid of Hayat Bakshi Begum.

The mortuary bath, which stands opposite the tomb of Muhammad Quli, was built by Sultan Quli to facilitate the ritual washing of the bodies of the dead kings and others of the royal family before they were carried to their final resting place. The practice followed was to bring the body out of the fort, through the Banjara Gate, to this bath, before carrying it away for burial with the ritualistic pomp that was required to mark the occasion. A large number of people, fond subjects, friends and relatives attended. The bath is one of the finest existing specimens of ancient Persian or Turkish baths.

The Qutb Shahis built a number of masjids all over Golkonda and Hyderabad, and almost every tomb has a masjid adjacent. The biggest and the grandest such masjid is by the mausoleum of Hayat Bakshi Begum. Popularly known as the great masjid of the Golkonda tombs, it was built in 1666 A.D. Fifteen cupolas decorate the roof and the prayer-hall is flanked by two lofty minarets. The impression, as a whole, is one of majesty and splendour. The inscriptions in the masjid are in calligraphic art.

Hayat Bakshi Begum was the daughter of Muhammed Quli Qutb Shah, the fifth sultan, the wife of Sultan Muhammed

Qutb Shah, the sixth sultan and the mother of Abdullah Qutb Shah, the seventh sultan. She was affectionately known as "*Ma Saheba*" (Revered Mother). The tomb-garden of the sultans of Golkonda was known as "*Lagar-e-Faiz Athar*" (a place for bountiful entertainment) in the days of the Qutb Shahi rulers, for some item or song or dance or even an occasional play was staged here every evening, free of cost, to entertain the poor.

CHOWMAHALLA PALACE

Chowmahalla Palace or Chowmahallatuu (4 Palaces), is a palace of the Nizams of Hyderabad state. It was the seat of the Asaf Jahi dynasty and was the official residence of the Nizams of Hyderabad while they ruled their state. The palace was built by Nizam Salabat Jung. The palace remains the property of Barkat Ali Khan Mukarram Jah, heir of the Nizams.

The place is named *chowmahalla*, which means four palaces. The word *char*, and its variation *chau*, means four and the word *mahal*means palace in Urdu and Hindi. It is more likely derived from Farsi words, as it was the official language of the Hyderabad State at the time. All ceremonial functions including the accession of the Nizams and receptions for the Governor-General were held at this palace.

The palace is located in the old city in Hyderabad near the Charminar.

The UNESCO Asia Pacific Merit award for cultural heritage conservation was presented to Chowmahalla Palace on 15 March 2010. UNESCO representative Takahiko Makino formally handed over the plaque and certificate to Princess Esra, former wife and GPA holder of Prince Mukarram Jah Bahadur.

History

While Salabat Jung initiated its construction in 1750, it was completed by the period of Afzal ad-Dawlah, Asaf Jah V between 1857 and 1869.

The palace is unique for its style and elegance. Building of the palace began in the late 18th century and over the decades a synthesis of many architectural styles and influences emerged.

The palace consists of two courtyards as well as he grand Khilwat (the Dharbar Hall), fountains and gardens. The palace originally covered 45 acres (180,000 m), but only 12 acres (49,000 m) remain today.

The palace was restored between 2005 and 2010 under the patronage of Princess Esra.

Southern Courtyard

Chowmahalla Palace interior with chandeliers

This is the oldest part of the palace, and has four palaces Afzal Mahal, Mahtab Mahal, Tahniyat Mahal and Aftab Mahal. It was built in the neo-classical style.

Northern courtyard

This part has *Bara Imam*, a long corridor of rooms on the east side facing the central fountain and pool that once housed the administrative wing and *Shishe-Alat*, meaning mirror image.

It has Mughal domes and arches and many Persian elements like the ornate stucco work that adorn the Khilwat Mubarak. These were characteristic of buildings built in Hyderabad at the time.

Opposite the Bara Imam is a building that is its shishe or mirror image. The rooms were once used as guest rooms for officials accompanying visiting dignitaries.

Khilwat Mubarak

This is heart of Chowmahalla Palace. It is held in high esteem by the people of Hyderabad, as it was the seat of the Asaf Jahi dynasty. The grand pillared Durbar Hall has a pure marble platform on which the Takht-e-Nishan or the royal seat was laid. Here the Nizams held their durbar and other religious and symbolic ceremonies. The 19 spectacular Chandeliers of Belgian crystal recently reinstalled to recreate the lost splendor of this regal hall.

Clock Tower

The clock above the main gate to Chowmahalla Palace is affectionately called Khilwat Clock. It has been ticking away for around 251 years. An expert family of clock repairers winds the mechanical clock every week.

Council Hall

This building housed a rare collection of manuscripts and priceless books.The Nizam often met important officials and dignitaries here. Today it is a venue for temporary exhibitions from the treasures of the Chowmahalla Palace Collection of the bygone era.

Roshan Bangla

The sixth Nizam is believed to have lived here and the building was named after his mother Roshan Begum.

The present Nizam (Barkat Ali Khan Mukarram Jah) and his family decided to restore the Chowmahalla Palace and open it to the public in January 2005. It took over 5 years to document and restore the palaces of the first courtyard to its former glory. The palace also has a collection of vintage cars like the Rolls Royce, which were used by the Nizam Kings. (Credit: Nikhil Arya Linga)

FALAKNUMA PALACE

Falaknuma is a palace in Hyderabad, Telangana, India. It belonged to the Paigah family, and was later owned by the Nizam of Hyderabad. It is on a 32-acre (13 ha) area in Falaknuma, 5 kilometers from Charminar. It was built by Nawab Sir Viqar-ul-Umra - Prime Minister of Hyderabad and the uncle & brother-in-law of the sixth Nizam. *Falak-numa* means "Like the Sky" or "Mirror of the Sky" in Urdu.

Design

An English architect designed the palace. The foundation stone for the construction was laid by Sir Vicar on 3 March 1884; he was the maternal grandson of Mir Akbar Ali Khan Sikander Jah, Asaf Jah III of Hyderabad. It took nine years to complete the construction and furnish the palace. Sir Vicar moved into the *Gol Bangla* and *Zanana Mahel* of the Falaknuma Palace in December 1890 and closely monitored the finishing work at the *Mardana* portion. It is made completely with Italian marble with stained-glass windows and covers an area of 1,011,500 square feet..

The palace was built in the shape of a scorpion with two stings spread out as wings in the north. The middle part is occupied by the main building and the kitchen, *Gol Bangla*, *Zenana Mehal*, and harem quarters stretch to the south. The Nawab was an avid traveler, and his influences show in the architecture, which combines Italian and Tudor influences.

History

Sir Viqar-ul-Umra, the Prime Minister of Hyderabad, used the palace as his private residence until the palace was handed over to the 6th Nizam of Hyderabad around 1897–1898. His monogram is on the furniture, walls and ceiling of the palace.

The palace was built and furnished at a cost of four million rupees, which necessitated borrowing money from the Bank of Bengal. In the spring of 1897, the sixth Nizam of Hyderabad Mir Mahbub Ali Khan was invited to stay at the palace. He extended his stay to a week, then a fortnight, and then a month, which prompted Sir Viqar to offer it to him. The Nizam accepted but paid some of the value of the palace; the Paigah family maintains that around 20 lakh rupees was paid.

The Nizam used the palace as a guest house for the royal guests visiting the kingdom of Hyderabad. The list of royal visitors included King George V, Queen Mary, Edward VIII and Tsar Nicholas II.

The palace fell into disuse after the 1950's. The last important guest was the President of India, Dr. Rajendra Prasad, in 1951.

The palace was then restored after being leased by the Taj Group of Hotels; the restoration, which began in 2010, was managed by Princess Esra, the first wife of Mukarram Jah.

Palace architecture

One of the highlights of the palace is the state reception room, where the ceiling is decorated with frescoes. The ballroom contains a two-ton manually operated organ said to be the only one of its kind in the world

The palace has 60 rooms and 22 halls. It has considerable collections of the Nizam's artifacts including paintings, statues, furniture, manuscripts, books, an extensive jade collection, and Venetian chandeliers. It has a library with a carved walnut roof, a replica of the one at Windsor Castle; it had an extensive collection of Qurans. The dining hall can seat 101 guests. The chairs are made of carved rosewood with green leather upholstery. Burroughs and Watts from England designed two identical billiards tables, one of which is in Buckingham Palace and the other in the palace's billiards room.

The palace was the private property of the Nizam family, and not normally open to the public, until 2000.

Renovation into a luxury hotel

In 2010, Taj Hotels started renovating and restoring the palace. The renovated hotel was opened in November 2010.

BIRLA MANDIR

Birla Mandir (Birla Temple) refers to different Hindu temples or Mandirs built by the Birla family, in different cities. All these temples are magnificently built, some of them in white marble or in sandstone. The temples are generally located in a prominent location, carefully designed to accommodate a large number of visitors. The worship and discourses are well organized. The first one was built in 1939 in Delhi collectively by Ghanshyamdas Birla and his brothers, as well his father. Later temples have been built by, and are managed by different branches of the family.

The Birla temples in Delhi and Bhopal were intended to fill a void. Delhi, even though it was the capital of India, did not have any notable temples. During the Mughal period, temples with shikharas were prohibited until the late Mughal period. The Delhi temple, located at a prominent spot was designed to be lofty and spacious, suitable for congregational worship or discourses. Although built using modern technology, it confirmed with the Nagar style. The Delhi, Banaras and the Bhopal temple use a modern style.

The later temples are built of marble or sandstone and are constructed in the classical (Chandela or Chaulukya) style of 10-12th century. The Saraswati temple, in the BITS Pilani campus is one of the very few Sarasvati temples built in modern times. It is said to be a replica of the Kandariya Mahadeva Temple temple of Khajuraho; however it is built of white marble and adorned with not only images of gods, but also philosophers and scientists. The Gwalior Sun temple is a replica of the famous Sun Temple of Konark, as it would have appeared before the collapse of the main tower. Anne Hardgrove states:

A national chain of the "Birla temples," temples of grandiose scale and design, have become major landmarks and part of the cityscapes of Indian urban life in the late twentieth century. The Birla temples exist in conjunction with other large industrial and philanthropic ventures of the wealthy Birla family, including major institutions of technology, medicine, and education. ...

Birla temples have redefined religion to conform to modern ideals of philanthropy and humanitarianism, combining the worship of a deity with a public institution that contributes to civil society. The architectural forms of the two newest Birla temples (*Jaipur and Kolkata*) incorporate innovative, dual-purpose structures into the temple design that alter temple practices to reflect the concerns of modern public culture in a religious site.

BHONGIR FORT

Bhongir Fort is a Fort located in Bhongir, Yadadri Bhuvanagiri District, Telangana, India. This fort was ruled and renovated by Musunuri Nayaks. It is located on a huge rock at a commanding height.

History

The Bhongir fort adorns the place from the time it was built in 10th century. Bhongir Fort was built on an isolated monolithic rock by the Western Chalukya ruler Tribhuvanamalla Vikramaditya VI in the year 1076 and was thus named after him as Tribhuvanagiri, later it was called as Bhuvanagiri.

Some of the inscriptions found in the fort were in Kannada and Telugu language highlighting the lifestyle of the people of that era.

The inscriptions, the architecture and some sculptures found in the fort reveal that the fort was ruled by the Chalukya dynasty for a long time and then by the Kakatiya dynasty. The stone wall, the steps through the granite archways and the crumbling stucco ruins of the later age, still adorn the place.

Somewhere in 15th century, the fort was ceded to the Bahamani Sultans and then was taken over by a local governor. The Qutub Shahis' used the fort as a prison for those who aspired to snatch their throne. During the time of the British, the fort escaped their attention and was not occupied. Bhuvanagirigir was much ignored after the downfall of the Nizams at the time of communist revolution in the late 1940s.

The Fort

Bhongir sits on a unique egg-shaped rock hill more than 500 feet high. The steps from the bottom of the hill to the top are still intact; at the beginning of the steps there is a Hanuman Temple with two entry points protected by huge rocks, so the fort was considered practically impregnable by invading armies. The splendid historical fort with the awe-inspiring rock and the aesthetically fortified courts which have stood the ravages of time stir the imagination of tourists. A moat that encircles the fort, a vast underground chamber, trap doors, an armoury, stables, ponds, wells etc., make for fascinating viewing. The view from the top of the surrounding of the neighbouring area. The fort is associated with the rule of the heroic queen Rudramadevi and the countryside is simply breathtaking. The Bala Hisar or citadel on the top of the hill gives a bird's eye view. Rumour has it that there once was an underground corridor connecting Bhongir Fort to Golconda Fort.

WARANGAL FORT

Warangal Fort, in Warangal district, Telangana in India. Appears to have existed since at least the 12th century when it was the capital of the Kakatiya dynasty. The fort has four ornamental gates, known as Kakatiya Kala Thoranam, that originally formed the entrances to a now ruined great Shiva temple. The Kakatiyan arch has been adopted and officially incorporated into the Emblem of Telangana after the state bifurcation. The Fort is included in the "tentative list" of UNESCO World Heritage Site. The Monument was submitted by the Permanent Delegation of India to UNESCO on 10/09/2010.

History

Initially, Warangal was under the rule of the Yadava kings in the 8th century; in the 12th century, it came under the control of the Kakatiya dynasty. Although precise dating of its construction and subsequent enhancements is uncertain, historians and archaeologists generally agree that an earlier brick-walled structure was replaced with stone by Ganapatideva, who died in 1262, and that he was succeeded by his daughter Rudrama Devi, who ruled until 1289, and then her grandson Prataparudra II, whose reign came to be known as a "Golden Age". Twenty years later his kingdom was conquered by the Sultans of Delhi.

Statue of Rudrama Devi, one of the rulers of the Kakatiya dynasty and builder of the fort complex

Ganapatideva, Rudramadevi, and Prataparudra II all added to the fort's height, building gateways, square bastions, and additional circular earthen walls. This places the construction towards the end of the Kakatiya period .

In 1309, Malik Kafur, the general of Alauddin Khalji, attacked the fort with a large force of 100,000 men and surrounded it. Prataparudra II and his people secured themselves within the formidable fort and battled bravely for many months with the invading army. As the siege could not be lifted for more than six months, Prataparudra II agreed to a truce with Kafur, as a result of which he gave in reparation all the wealth that he had accumulated. This included the famous Koh-i-Noor diamond. This siege was chronicled by Amir Khusrow, who described how the fortifications consisted of a strong outer hardened mud structure with a deep ditch in front that had to be filled with dirt before the army could surmount it. The inner fortress was built of stone and surrounded by a moat that the Muslim soldiers swam across. The fort as described by Khusrow corresponds to the two inner circles of fortifications that exist today. When Kafur finally left the fort in March 1310, he carried away the bounty on 2,000 camels. The conditions of forging peace with the Delhi Sultanate included a clause that Pratapa Rudra would pay an annual tribute and that he would bow every day towards Delhi as a tributary king denoting his subordinate status to the Sultan of Delhi. After Kafur's departure, Pratapa Rudra started ruling again, and during this time some of his vassal chieftains had declared themselves independent rulers of their fiefdoms. But in 1311 Pratapa Rudra had to support the Sultan in invading the Pandyan kingdom, which he did, and he also succeeded in getting the vassals back under his control.

Again in 1318, as Pratapa Rudra had willfully ignored paying the annual tribute to the Sultans of Delhi, Warangal Fort was attacked and held in siege. The superior military power (including superior implements to lob stone missiles and many other similar tools) of the Sultan's army again forced Pratapa Rudra to sue for peace. The invaders had even put up a 450 feet (140 m) earthen ramp across the moat which enabled them to breach the stone walls of the fort and capture it. He again paid a huge tribute to the Sultan in the form of a contingent of horses and elephants, which became an annual fee to be paid to the Delhi Sultanate. After he sued for peace, the Sultan bestowed on him a "mace, a decorated robe (qaba) and a parasol". And again he had to bow towards the imperial capital of Delhi as a mark of his vassal status.

When in 1320 Pratapa Rudra again defaulted on his annual

payment to the Delhi sultans, the then ruler of Delhi who had replaced Khalji, Sultan Ghiyath al-Din Tughluq, sent his son Ulugh Khan to recover the dues.

For a third and final time, the fort was attacked by Sultan Muhammad bin Tughluq (r. 1325–1351), who held siege over the fort.

Due to internal dissension, Ulugh Khan had to retreat to Devagiri. After a temporary respite, Ulugh Khan came back in 1323 with 65,000 mounted soldiers carrying archery, attacked the fort, and plundered and destroyed the capital. In keeping with that tradition, the Muslim general Ulugh Khan ordered destruction of the great Svayambhusiva Temple where the State deity had been deified.

All that is now visible of the temple are remnants scattered around the fort. Then the Tughluqan authorities built an enormous mosque to one side of the fort, which has since been demolished. Pratapa Rudra, who had surrendered and was sent to Delhi, died on the way on the banks of the Godavari River. It is said that he committed suicide in 1323. The capital of Warangal was then renamed as Sultanpur, and from 1324 to 1332 imperial coins were minted there. The [Delhi Sultanate managed to hold Sultanpur until 1335, when the local Nayakas (72 of the chieftains) formed a union and took control.

The fort then came under the control of the Qutb Shahi dynasty of Golconda and later under the rule of the Nizam of Hyderabad.

Later modifications to the fort were made between the 15th and 17th centuries, mainly with the addition of barbicans to the four gates in the stone wall and the creation of gates in the outer earthen wall.

Remnants of the structure can be seen today near the town of Warangal, which was the Kakatiya capital.

The Archaeological Survey of India has listed the ruins as a Monument of National Importance.

Features

Ruins within the main fort complex

Warangal Fort is laid out in three concentric circular walls with defensive fortifications. The first structure, built during the reign of Rudrama Devi, was in the form an earthen embankment 1.5 miles (2.4 km) in diameter. A moat of about 150 feet (46 m) width was dug around this wall, forming the outer limits of the fort during the reign of the Kakatiya rulers. Another wall built to protect the fort after the earthen wall and the moat was a fortified inner stone wall of about 0.75 miles (1.21 km) in diameter.

It was the central part of the Kakatiya capital, called the fort. This wall was built with dressed huge granite stone blocks of very large dimensions. These stones were not in any regular shape, but were closely fitted without using any type of mortar. During the reign of Rudrama Devi the height of the wall was increased to 29 feet (8.8 m) from the structure which had been built earlier by Ganapati Dev. The wall has been fortified with 45 very large rectangular bastions (also known as towers), which measure 40–60 feet (12–18 m) on a side; they extend beyond the face of the wall up to the waters of the moat. There are also 18 stone steps laid over a gradual slope built on the inner slopes of the earthen wall as an access to the ramparts.

As these steps covered the entire central area of the fort they permitted the soldiers easy and quick access in times of war from any location in the fort, including the top of the ramparts. The king, Pratapa Rudra, had used these steps to go to the rampart in 1318, attired with qaba to bow towards Delhi, in honour of the Sultan.

There is also a third ring of fortification in the form of a mud wall of 12.5 kilometres (7.8 mi) diameter that encloses the present city of Warangal.

Ruins in the fort

The area within the fort has an axial road laid in an east-west direction where there is now some human habitation. The central part of the fort has been identified as the archaeological zone where the ruins of a great Shiva temple are now seen with only the freestanding "entrance portals" or gates on the four sides. Each gate has twin pillars with angled brackets over which lies the huge lintel; the height of this gate is 10 metres (33 ft). The gates have extensive intricate carvings of "lotus buds, looped garlands, mythical animals, and birds with foliated tails". The carvings do not include any religious symbols, which is said to be the reason for its preserved condition and not getting destroyed by the Muslim invaders. Of the four gateways (local name*charkamou*), the northern and southern ends are 480 feet (150 m) apart. The eastern and western gates are a distance of 433 feet (132 m) from each other.

While the Shiva temple has been completely destroyed, there are many ruins of "wall slabs, brackets and ceiling panels", some of which are exhibited now in an outdoor museum. There are still some standing pillars ("temple spoilia") that the Bahmanis earlier used to build a mosque, which remained incomplete.

The original deity of the temple was a linga with the four faces of Shiva, which is now deified in a separate shrine to the south of the fort complex, where regular worship is offered. Archaeological excavations in the area have also unearthed many small shrines, built in a series, deified with a votive linga.

Seen within 150 metres (490 ft) of the archaeological zone is the Kush Mahal, which is a public hall built in the 14th century by the Delhi Sultans, who had captured the fort. The mahal, which is rectangular in shape, is built with huge sloping walls, sliced by six arched openings on each of its sides. There was once a timber roof over this mahal, supported by five transverse arches built of stones.

There are approach steps on the northeast corner that provide access to the top of the structure, which has scenic views of the entire fort complex.

Within the southern quarter of the archaeological zone is a big water tank. Inside this tank is a distinctive natural rock formation that protrudes above the water surface. This is called locally as *Orugallu* (meaning: single rock) in Telugu, giving the name "Warangal" to the fort. A small temple is built over this rock. There are many other temples and water ponds in the entire fort complex. There are also three large granaries close to the south gate of the fort.

Just outside the central fort, the mud wall, which is the second circle of the fort complex in the northwestern part, has within it the Lanja gudi ('gudi' means "shrine"), which consists of three small temples; but the linga deities have been removed and are seen scattered nearby.

There are many inscriptions on the ruins of the wall of the main temple recording the gift of a Kakatiya king, on pillars, on a stone outside the fort, and at many more places, all in the Telugu language.

KHAMMAM FORT

Khammam Fort is a fort in the city of Khammam, Telangana, India constructed by Musunuri Kamma Kings. It served as an impregnable citadel during various regimes of different dynasties, including the Qutb Shahi's and Asaf Jahis. The fort was situated in a very vast area in the heart of the City of Khammam. It was notified as a protected monument by the Archaeology Department several decades ago. Despite decades of neglect, the historical edifice, which once flourished with regal opulence, presents its alluring charm due to its architectural splendor.

Etymology

The historical records show that the name was "Kammamet." Mett or Mettu means fort in Telugu language.

Construction

Kammamet was built by Musunuri Kings. Several inscriptions were discovered in the surrounding areas of Khammam and Krishna districts of Musunuri Kings dating back to 10th and 11th century A.D.

Kammamet slowly became an independent territory within the kingdom of Kakatiya Kings for Musunuri Kings.

75 Telugu speaking feudatories of the region under the leadership of Musunuri Kings fought for 10 long years to unify the Telugu land and succeeded in repulsing them out of country.

Architecture & Significant Features

- This Fort is located in an area of 4 Sq. miles in the heart of the City of Khammam on top of a massive granite Hill. It is surrounded by a huge rock wall averaging between 40 and 80 feet(13 to 25 Meters) in height and 15 to 20 feet(4.5 to 6 Meters) in width. There are steps from each buruju (bastion) to enter into the fort. The Fort was considered practically impregnable by invading armies.
- A number of balconies and windows are constructed along the wall in order to use the artillery during wartime. It has a capacity of mounting at least 60 cannons at a time.
- The fort 10 large gates most of them in poor shape now. Each gate has cannons mounted on them along with a water pot made of rocks. They are built such that an impact of a cannonball could not break it.
- The main entrance is a 30 foot tall entrance known as the Khilla darwaza(meaning fort gate in Urdu). It has 2

cannons on either side of the entrance. One of them still mounted with a head. They are now partially destroyed due to the negligence of the archeology department.

- The east gate or the secondary entrance is equally large and is popularly known as the Raathi Darwaza(meaning stone entrance in Urdu) or Potha Darwaza.
- All other gates are smaller than the main entrance and could have been constructed to avoid large cavalries to enter the fort in case of an attack.
- A huge rainwater catchment system and well have been constructed on the Khilla during the period of Zafar-ud-doula, well known for construction of tanks during Qutb shahi dynasty. This massive tank is now known as the 'Zafar well'. It is 60 feet X 30 feet stepped well with a bridge across it for men and horses to move around. He also built the walls using Bricks and limestone along the fort.
- As soon as we enter the Khilla darwaza, one can see the Fort at a distance of 300 feet. There are small steps carved out of this hill to reach the top of the Hill fort. They are later renovated with railings for the steps by the Tourism department and Archaeological Survey of India in 2005 during the 1000 year celebrations of this historical fort. A lot of small gates known as 'Dalohiswar' are all around the walls of the fort.
- Fort has at least 15 bastions constructed with two massive walls as a military strategy to take the impact of the cannonballs and to counter the enemy from the top. A 15 foot deep trench is dug in some places for the army to store and use as a hiding place.
- The huge blocks of stone used for the walls are as long as 10 feet and are believed to be transported using elephants and men. No mud or limestone is used in this huge wall and the rocks are tightly placed and leaving the viewers amazed by the construction
- A permanent Gallows has been erected on this prominent hill fort, where the estimated seat of justice could have

been inside the fort. The platform is made of Stone and appears like a well, due to which the locals call this 'Nethi bhavi' ('meaning Ghee well).This stone structure could be seen from allover the city of khammam.

- The fort is believed to have a secret tunnels to the Warangal Fort with multiple entrances in different locations at the fort. One such entrance is 10 feet in diameter and the steps to enter the tunnel are closed due to damage over the years. The local folklore includes stories about valuables being transferred between the kings from here using the secret passages and escaping enemy attacks through them.

Culture

This Fort appears to be a replicate the cultures of both Hindu and Muslim rulers who ruled this fort city.

The Lakshmi Narasimha swami temple in Brahmin bazar, Sri Ramalingeshwara temple is one of the oldest shivalayam(Shiva temple) are some of the oldest Hindu temples in Telangana and are older than the fort itself.

During the Qutb shahi dynasty, many new places of worship have been constructed in and around the fort such as the Khilla masjid.

Encroachments

The fort, once mighty bastion of royal dynasties, continues to face further encroachment threat due to lack of proper monitoring mechanism.Large settlements occupied the areas in and around the fort due to the lack of proper monitoring of encroachments. Destruction of the granite hill and construction of houses continues till today around the fort area.

Development

The historic Khammam fort, a living testimony to the majestic grandeur and architectural marvel of the bygone era, is poised to get a face lift with the government departments drawing up grand plans to beautify and develop the majestic edifice.Illumination of the fort, including installation of solar streetlights atop the fort, introduction of the sound and light show at the historical edifice and development of a park at the entrance of the fort, are some of the initiatives in the pipeline.With the Telangana government laying renewed focus on the historical edifices of architectural significance, the government departments turned their attention on beautifying the Khammam fort and safeguarding the protected monument from future encroachments.A proposal to develop a park and set up a canteen besides illuminating the fort at an estimated cost of Rs. 5 crore has already been submitted to the government, says Suman Chakravarthi, District Tourism Officer, Khammam. The plan also envisages provision of amenities and introduction of sound and light show at the fort on the lines of the Golconda Fort in Hyderabad, he elaborates.A plan is on the anvil to install solar streetlights at the fort, says G. S. V. Prasad, District Manager, New and Renewable Energy Development Corporation.Recently Minister for Roads & Buildings Tummala Nageswara Rao has mooted the proposal to set up solar streetlights at the fort well before the next Independence Day celebrations in 2017.

SITA RAMACHANDRASWAMY TEMPLE, BHADRACHALAM

The Sri Sita Ramachandraswamy temple is a South Indian Hindu temple dedicated to Rama, the seventh incarnation of the god Vishnu. It is located on the shores of the Godavari River in the town of Bhadrachalam, a part of the Bhadradri Kothagudem districtin Telangana state. Often simply referred to as Bhadrachalam or Bhadradri, the temple is considered one of the *Divya Kshetrams*of Godavari and is also revered as Dakshina Ayodhya. According to the legend, Vishnu appeared to Meru's son Bhadra as Rama to answer the latter's prayers. However, Vishnu forgot that Rama was a mortal human and appeared as Vaikuntha Rama with four hands. Sita and Lakshmana form part of the temple's moolavar.

The self-manifested moolavar was discovered in the 17th century by Pokala Dhammakka, a tribal woman living in Bhadrareddypalem. After she built a mandapam for the idols, Bhadrachalam's tehsildar Kancherla Gopanna constructed this temple during the reign of Abul Hasan Qutb Shah. After Gopanna, Tumu Lakshmi Narasimha Dasu and Varada Ramadasu looked after the temple's rituals. Bhadrachalam follows the Vaishnavite Pancharatra Agama tradition, and its system of worship is modelled on that of the Ranganathaswamy temple in Srirangam. The temple has four entrances; the Rajagopuram is located at the northern entrance, which is called the Vaikuntha Dwaram. The temple houses a number of sub-shrines and a few mandapams.

Bhadrachalam is notable for its principal deity Vaikuntha Rama, a form of Rama not found anywhere else in the country. According to the *Brahma Purana*, the temple's deity is capable of imparting knowledge to those who worship him. Gopanna used Bhadrachalam as a centre of the Bhajan tradition to spread awareness of the Vaishnavite tradition. The annual Brahmotsavam is the biggest festival celebrated in Bhadrachalam; the key event is the *Sri Sitarama Thirukalyana Mahotsavam*, or the marriage of Rama and Sita on the eve of Sri Rama Navami. Other important festivals celebrated in Bhadrachalam are Vaikuntha Ekadashi, Vasanthotsavam, and Vijayadashami.

Legend

According to Hindu legend, in the Treta Yuga, Rama (avatar of the god Vishnu), along with his consort Sita and brother Lakshmana, stayed in the Dandaka forest as a part of their fourteen-year exile. Due to Rama's grace, a stone turned into a human called Bhadra, who was considered the son of Mount Meru. Devoted to Rama, Bhadra later met the sage Narada, who initiated an *upadesam* (instruction) of the *Rama Taraka mantra*. Bhadra mediated and chanted the mantra on the banks of the Godavari River for several years. Pleased, Rama promised to return to meet Bhadra when he had found Sita, who had been abducted by the demon king Ravana. However, Rama failed to fulfill his promise in his lifetime.

Later, Vishnu was pleased with Bhadra's devotion and appeared before Bhadra in the form of Rama. In a hurry, Vishnu forgot that Rama was a mortal with two arms and appeared with his four celestial arms. Rama in upper arms held a shankha (conch) and the Sudarshana Chakra (discus) and a bow and an arrow in his lower hands. Sita was seated on his left thigh and Lakshmana stood to his left. All three faced west towards the Godavari River. Rama held the conch in his right upper hand in contrast to Vishnu, with the intention of giving salvation to Bhadra.

Rama turned Bhadra into a hillock; the images of the deities in the same postures manifested at its summit. The hillock was referred to as Bhadrachalam or Bhadradri ("Bhadra's hill"). The central icon of Rama is referred by various epithets. Since Rama descended from Vaikuntha (Vishnu's abode) and manifested there, he was called "Vaikuntha Rama". As the deity is four-armed like Vishnu (Narayana), he was named "Rama Narayana". The trio of deities together signified the aspects of the sacred sound *Om*, which earned Rama the sobriquet of "Om-kara Rama".

History

In the 17th century CE, Pokala Dhammakka, a tribal woman living in Bhadrareddypalem, found the central icon of Rama in an anthill. She dissolved the anthill using the water from the Godavari River. With the help of the villagers, Dhammakka constructed a mandapam (hall) and offered prayers to the deities. During the reign of Abul Hasan Qutb Shah (1672-1686), Kancherla Gopanna served as the tehsildar(revenue officer) of Bhadrachalam. Gopanna was given the title of Ramadas (Rama's servant) by Kabirdas, a Muslim saint who was impressed with his charity. Following the Shah's orders, Gopanna enforced the Jaziya tax, a penalty designed to force Hindus to adopt Islam. Observing the dilapidated state of the temple, Gopanna decided to build a temple for the deity by raising donations. In the initial attempt, Gopanna received harsh criticism from the local Hindus for enforcing the tax. Dejected by numerous rebuffs, Gopanna decided to use a portion of the tax collected to build the temple and face the consequences.

The temple was completed at a cost of nearly six lakh *varahas*. After learning the truth, the Shah was enraged, and Gopanna was summoned to the court. Gopanna explained that he never intended to misuse the treasury funds and planned to reimburse using donations he expected to receive in the future. The Shah ordered his soldiers to hang Gopanna if the sum was not repaid within twelve years, and imprisoned him. On the last day of the twelfth year, Rama and Lakshmana appeared in Shah's dream and repaid the entire sum in *Rama madas* (gold coins with Rama's inscriptions on them). When the Shah woke up, he saw real gold coins and released Gopanna. He gave Gopanna a pension for life and donated the area around Bhadrachalam as an endowment to the temple. Some scholars dismissed the idea of Rama paying the money, saying that the Shah had held a fair and impartial inquiry, found Gopanna innocent, and exonerated him with due Honour.

Years later, Tumu Lakshmi Narasimha Dasu of Guntur and his friend Varada Ramadasu of Kanchipuram offered prayers daily at Bhadrachalam and spent their life there. After Varada Ramadasu's death, Narasimha Dasu carried his corpse into the Godavari and died by drowning.

The temple was a part of the Godavari district until the end of the Visalandhra movement, after which the town was merged into Khammam district in 1956. The temple's maintenance and administration were undertaken by the endowment ministry of the Government of Andhra Pradesh in 1958. Repairs were made to the temple in 1960 under the supervision of the then-endowments minister Kalluri Chandramouli.

In August 1986 the temple faced a severe threat from flash floods in the Godavari River. The main streets and several structures, including cottages, were submerged in water for nearly five days. Many local people took shelter in the halls of the temple. The kalyana mandapam (marriage hall) was completely inundated except for its gopuram (temple tower). P. Seshacharyulu and other priests stayed in the temple and performed all the daily rituals without any interruption during the floods.

The Nizam of Hyderabad, Mir Osman Ali Khan during his time made a huge donation of Rs. 50,000 for this temple during his time.

During the Telangana movement, both the states of Telangana and Andhra Pradesh claimed that the Bhadrachalam temple belongs to their respective regions. Telangana politicians and activists stood firm on their stance and stated that they would not let Bhadrachalam be separated from the state. Bhadrachalam was retained in Telangana, and after reorganisation of districts in October 2016, the temple became a part of Bhadradri Kothagudem district.

The temple

The temple is divided into three parts. The first is believed to be the head of Bhadra, where a shrine is dedicated to him. Inside, on a rock structure, the supposed footprints of Rama can be seen. Thirunamam(a white clay) is applied to the rock so that the visitors can recognise it as Bhadra's head. The second part of the temple is the sanctum where the central icon resides on a place considered equivalent to Bhadra's heart. The third part is the Rajagopuram (main tower), which is located at Bhadra's feet.

The temple has four entrances; there are 50 steps to be climbed to reach the main entrance. In 1974, a huge door named the *Vaikuntha Dwaram* was built to ensure proper management of the visiting devotees. Directly opposite to the sanctum is a gold-plated dwajasthambam (flag post). It is made of panchaloha (a five-metal alloy), on which are carved images of Garuda, the vehicle of Vishnu.On the top of the vimana of the sanctum is an eight-faced Sudarshana Chakra with a thousand corners, that was engraved by Gopanna, who found it lying in the waters of the Godavari River. On the vimana, a miniature of the temple's deity can be seen. The entrance for devotees, who have purchased a special visit ticket, is towards the left of the sanctum. The regular visitors have to wait in a queue that leads straight into the sanctum. Housed in an area to the right of the sanctum are the festival icons of Rama, Sita, and Lakshmana, which are worshipped daily.

The central icon housed in the sanctum is considered *Swayambhu* (self-manifested). Rama is seated in a padmasana posture, with Sita seated on his lap. Rama's four hands hold the conch, disc, bow, and arrow. Lakshmana stands to his left.

On a taller hill, Gopanna installed and consecrated the icon of Ranganatha, a reclining form of Vishnu, which faces the south. The place is popularly known as *Ranganayakula Gutta* (hillock of Ranganatha). Opposite the Ranganatha sanctum is a temple dedicated to his consort Lakshmi Thayar. These two temples were included by Gopanna to follow the tradition of Srirangam Ranganathaswamy temple. The temple houses a number of other shrines. Hanuman has two shrines in the temple: the Abhayanjaneya temple at the river bank and the Dasanjaneya temple in the *Thiruveedhi* (divine passage) of Bhadrachalam. In the *Rajaveedhi* (royal passage) of the temple, a shrine of Govindaraja Swamy (a form of Vishnu) can be found where the festival icons of Bhadrachalam spend some time during the *Thiruveedhi utsavam* festival procession. On the way to the main temple from the river bank, a shrine is dedicated to Yogananda-Narasimha. The icon is believed to be *Swayambhu* and very powerful.

Next to the Lakshmi Thayar temple is the Rushya Mookham Exhibition centre. In the centre, the *Rama mada* coins given to the Shah, jewellery made by Gopanna for the deities, and other important items are housed. The jewellery includes the *chintaku patakam* (a necklace studded with rubies), *kirithas* (crowns), plaited decorations, and a *mutyala haramu* (chain of pearls). In the outer ambulatory passage of the temple, there is a hall called the *Nithyakalyana mandapam* or *kalyana mandapam*, intended for conducting the marriage festival of

Rama and Sita. On the Ranganayakula Gutta is a temple dedicated to the god Shiva, who is worshipped as *Ramalingeswaraswamy*. Near the *kalyana mandapam*, there is a hermitage named Govindaswamy matham where many saints stayed in the past.A huge hall named Mithila Stadium was built facing the Vaikuntha Dwaram. Its construction was initiated by Jalagam Vengala Rao and was completed at a cost of 3.8 million.The icons worshipped by Narasimha Dasu are housed in the Ambasatram, which is located at the southern end of the temple. Here, food is served to the devotees visiting the temple.

Religious practices

According to *Ramayana* and other sacred texts, Ranganatha was the *Kuladevata* (tutelary deity) of Rama's clan, the Ikshvaku dynasty. Hence, Gopanna wanted this temple to implement all the traditions and guidelines of the Srirangam temple dedicated to Ranganatha. For the same reason, he invited five families from Srirangam who knew the *Pancharatra Agama* traditions to Bhadrachalam. With their help, the system of worship followed in the Srirangam temple was implemented here. Narasimha Dasu later introduced the *Dasavidhotsavams* (ten kinds of rituals), including *Nitya Kainkaryams* (daily rituals), *Vaarotsavams* (weekly rituals), *Pakshotsavams* (fortnightly rituals), and *Punarvasu utsavam* (rituals on the Punarvasu day).

The *suprabhata seva* (pre-dawn ritual) begins early in the morning at 4:00 am, followed by providing *Balabhoga* (minor food offerings) from 5:30 to 7:00 am. From 8:30 to 11:30, the regular *archana* (prayer) activities are held. *Rajabhogam* (main food offering) is served to the deity from 11:30 am to 12:00 noon; then the temple remains closed until 3:00 pm.From 3:00, the *archana* rituals continue, after which *darbar seva* (the king's court ritual) is performed from 7:00 to 8:00 pm. After a break to offer food to the deity from 8:30 to 9:00 pm, the temple is closed after performance of the *pavalimpu seva* (the sleeping ritual). *Abhisheka* (anointment) in the main sanctum is performed only to Rama's feet on the rock structure in Bhadra's temple.

This ritual is also performed to the deities in the Lakshmi, Anjaneya, and Yogananda Narasimha temple exclusively on every Friday, Tuesday, and Saturday, respectively. There are weekly, monthly, and fortnightly rituals performed in the temple apart from the annual ones. *Kalyanam* (marriage) and *Thiruveedhi utsavam* (procession festival) are performed at the Ranganayakula Gutta every year for its presiding deity Ranganatha.

Festivals

Vaikuntha Ekadashi

The Vaikuntha Ekadashi celebrations are based on the traditions followed in Srirangam. As per the *Bhadradri Kshetra Mahatyam*(Importance of Bhadradri) in the *Brahma Purana*, devotees seeking the blessings of Vaikuntha Rama on the annual festival day of Vaikuntha Ekadashi shall be granted salvation. The *Agama* text named *Paramapurusha Samhita* states that the devotees must watch Vishnu seated on the procession vehicle of Garuda proceeding from the North gate to fulfill their wish of gaining salvation.

As a prelude to Vaikuntha Ekadashi, *Teppotsavam* (the float festival) is celebrated during which a swan-shaped boat named *Hamsavahanam*is utilised for the procession of the utsava icons on the waters of the Godavari River. Teppotsavam is held at night under the light of electrical lighting and fireworks. The boat makes five circular rounds in the water, and nearly 26 people accompany the icons in the procession. On the day of Vaikuntha Ekadashi, the utsava idols of Rama, Sita, and Lakshmana are seated on Garudavahanam, and devotees pass through the Vaikuntha Dwaram. *Goda Kalyanam* and *Rathotsavam* (the chariot festival) form the other main important activities of the 21-day-long celebrations; the latter coincides with the Makar Sankranti festival.

Vasanthotsavam

Vasanthotsavam (festival of spring) is celebrated to mark the commencement of the preparations for the annual

Brahmotsavam (Grand celebration) festival. This festival coincides with Holi and involves the preparation of the *mutyala talambralu* (*talambralu* made of pearls and rice; *talambralu* is a mixture of rice and turmeric used in South-Indian marriage rituals). Natural pearls are mixed with rice grains, the husks of which have been removed with nails, and turmeric powder. This entire mixture is processed by hand. This mixture, with the addition of aromatic ingredients, is known as *Goti talambralu* (talamralu polished by nails).

The event begins with Vaishnava women gathering in the *Chitrakoota mandapam* hall in the temple's premises and participating in an initial prayer to the traditional grinding equipment. They powder the turmeric seeds using the traditional grinding equipment and use them in the preparation of the *Goti talambralu*. The icon of Rama is decorated using nine blocks of turmeric powder and other aromatic ingredients. The priests perform *Maha Kumbhaprokshana* (sanctification of the temple). The water used in the process, known as *Vasantha theertham*, is sprinkled on the devotees who then celebrate Holi. *Dolotsavam* (the swing ritual) is performed to conclude Vasanthotsavam by placing the festival icons in a golden cradle and singing lullabies.

Brahmotsavam

The chief temple festival is the twelve-day long annual Brahmotsavam festival (the *Vasantha Paksha Prayukta Srirama Navami Brahmotsavam*),celebrated during March—April. Rama Navami, the birthday of Rama, is the main event of the Brahmotsavam.According to the *Pancharatra Agama* rules, Rama's marriage with Sita is held on this day; the marriage is performed at a time that signifies the presence of the stars Punarvasu and Abhijit. This festival is formally referred to as *Sri Sitarama Thirukalyana Mahotsavam*.

Brahmotsavam is initiated by performing *Visesha Snapanam* (a special cleansing) of the festival icons followed by *Ankurarpanam* (the formal start), listening to the *Panchangam* dictation, and the *Thiruveedhi utsavam*. The *Dwajapata Bhadraka Mandala Lekhanam*, a flag made of white cloth with an image of Garuda, is prepared, and special prayers are performed. The Garuda image, whose eyes are covered with wax, has five colours in it. The flag is worshipped with hymns such as *Garudanyasam* and *Garuda Dhyanam*. After placing the flag at the feet of the temple's central icon, it is taken to the Vedi (fire altar) and placed on a heap of rice. The procedure is completed by performing Abhisheka (libation) to the flag with sixteen kalashas containing sacred water. This ritual is referred to as *Garudadhivasam* (invitating Garuda).

After *Garudadhivasam*, the priests perform *Dwajarohanam* (flag hoisting) and start a special fire ritual. Brahmotsavam continues with the *Edurukolu* (welcoming the bridegroom) event before proceeding to the marriage. The Shah, after releasing Gopanna from jail, started the tradition of sending pearls and silk robes as gifts to Rama and Sita on the eve of the marriage conducted in the temple. This tradition continued uninterrupted throughout the Qutb Shahi reign, and all succeeding governments. These pearls are used along with the *Goti talambralu* in the *Thirukalyana Mahotsavam*.

The mangala sutra necklace used in this marriage ceremony contains three coin-sized gold discs. According to Telugu tradition, one disc pertains to Dasharatha, Rama's father, and the second one to Janaka, Sita's father. The third one pertains to Gopanna, who considered Sita as his daughter. This three-disc mangala sutra provided by Gopanna is only available in Bhadrachalam and is used even today. After completion of the marriage ceremony, *Mahapattabishekam* (the coronation ceremony) and *Teppotsavam* are held. Brahmotsavam ends with the completion of *Sripushpayagam* (flower worship).

Vijayadashami

The ten-day Dussehra is one of the key festivals celebrated in Bhadrachalam. The Ramayana is read for ten days daily during the ritual of a yagna, which ends on the tenth day and is referred to as Vijayadashami. The rituals are performed in the Lakshmi Thayar temple according to the rules of the Pancharatra Agama. On Vijayadashami, the nijaroopa darshanam (true form darshan) of Lakshmi Thayar attracts thousands of devotees. In the morning, Abhisheka and Sahasranama archana (recital of a thousand attributes) are performed to Lakshmi Thayar.

The key events of the Dussehra celebrations are the marriage and coronation of Rama followed by special prayers to his weapons and the Shami tree (prosopis cineraria). After the completion of the yagna, Rama's idol is dressed like that of an emperor and is carried out in a procession on the vehicles of Gaja (elephant) and Aswa (horse). As a part of the weapon worship, Rama's conch, disc, bow, and mace are used. Arrows representing the powers of the vedic deities Indra, Yama, Varuna, and Kubera are also made a part of the worship. The event ends with the traditional Ramlila ceremony conducted at night.

Other festivals

The other prominent festivals celebrated at Bhadrachalam are Hanuman Jayanti, Sabari Smruti Yatra, and Dhammakka Seva Yatra. Hanuman Jayanti is celebrated at the Dasanjaneya temple, with leaf worship and Thiruveedhi utsavam being the main events. Devotees mark the conclusion of their Hanuman Deeksha by untying the *Irumudi* (sacred bundle) before Rama and offering it at the Dasanjaneya temple. For Sabari Smruti Yatra, members of local tribes sport distinctive head gear and clothing. They sing and dance to the drum beats and display their archery skills.

The main event of Dhammakka Seva Yatra is the marriage of Govindaraja Swamy and his consorts. Special performers among the members of tribes from 29 mandals around Bhadrachalam offer floral tributes to Dhammakka's statue. They offer talambralu to the deity in addition to flowers and fruits, and perform traditional dances. Apart from these, the jayanthi utsavam (birthday) of Gopanna and Narasimha Dasu are also celebrated annually.

Religious significance

Bhadrachalam is often referred to as Dakshina Ayodhya ("Southern Ayodhya"); Ayodhya being the capital of Rama. The iconography of the Vaikuntha Rama form of Rama, is unique and not found anywhere else in the country. The *Brahma Purana* makes special mention of the temple's significance and adds that Vaikuntha Rama is capable of imparting knowledge to those who worship him at Bhadrachalam. The Hindu saints Adi Shankara and Thirumangai Alvar visited the temple and offered prayers to the deity. Bhadrachalam is considered as one of the *Divya Kshetrams* (special temples) that sit on the banks of the Godavari River. Hence, the river's Pushkaram and Maha Pushkaramare celebrated here along with others once every twelve years and 144 years, respectively.

As per legend, when a Muslim saint Kabir who was also a devotee of Rama, was once denied entry into the temple by the priests. The images of the temple disappeared for the moment. Ramadass who was there pleaded with the priests to let the saint inside the temple, after which the icons appeared again.

Gopanna used Bhadrachalam as a centre of the Bhajan tradition to spread awareness of the Vaishnavite tradition. This eventually led to the increase in the number of Rama temples in the Telugu-speaking states across the years, especially in villages. Gopanna's songs inspired Tyagaraja, another ardent devotee of Rama who composed several songs in Indian carnatic music. Tyagaraja revered Gopanna as his "personal hero", and he composed several songs modelled on songs written by Gopanna in praise of Vaikuntha Rama. He later inspired Narasimha Dasu, who composed songs in praise of Rama during his stay at Bhadrachalam. It helped Narasimha Dasu gain recognition as a true follower of Gopanna. The annual tradition of giving pearls and silk robes to Rama on the day of his marriage celebrations has been replicated at many other smaller temples dedicated to the deity.

GNANA SARASWATI TEMPLE, BASAR

Gnana Saraswati Temple is a Hindu temple of Goddess Saraswati located on the banks of Godavari River at Basar, Telangana, India. It is one of the two famous Saraswati temples in India, the other being in Jammu & Kashmir. Saraswati is the Hindu Goddess of knowledge and learning. Children are brought to the temple for the learning ceremony called as Akshara abyasam.

Basar is a census town in the nirmal district in the state of Telangana. It is about 30 km (19 mi) from Bhainsa,15.5 km (10 mi) from Dharmabad, 34.8 km (22 mi) from Nizamabad, 96.0 km (60 mi) from Nanded, 70 km (43 mi) from district headquarters Nirmal, and 205 km (127 mi) from Hyderabad.

History

According to Mahabharatha, Maharishi Vyas and his disciples and sage Viswamitra decided to settle down in a cool and serene atmosphere after the Kurukshetra War. In the quest for a peaceful abode, he came to Dandaka forest and, pleased with serenity of the region, selected this place. Since Maharishi Vyasa spent considerable time in prayers, the place was then called "Vasara" and turned into Basara due to the influence of the Marathi language in this region.

It is also believed that this temple is one of the three temples constructed near the confluence of the Manjira and Godavari rivers.

Historically, 'Bijialudu' a Karnataka king, who ruled the province of Nandagiri with Nanded as his capital in the sixth century, constructed the temple at Basara.

The Temple Today

Many pilgrims come to Gnana Saraswati Temple Basar to perform the "Akshara abhyasam" ceremony for the children before they start formal school education. The children perform the exercise of letters, and devote books, pens, pencils notebooks to the goddess of knowledge. The Puja at the temple starts at

4 am in morning with Abhishekam which carries on for an hour. At 5 o'clock they start the Alankarana whereby the new sarees are adorned to the goddesses. The whole atmosphere is very pious and pure. At 6 am, in the rays of the morning sun, the aarti starts at the temple after which the prasadam is given to the devotees.

Photo of the river Godavari, behind/adjacent to the temple, taken on 30 April 2011.

Special poojas and celebrations are held at the temple during Maha Shivaratri, beginning 15 days before (Vasantha Panchami) and continuing 3 days after the festival. Devi Navarathrulu is celebrated for ten days during Dasara.

The temple also has a Mahakali idol situated on the 1st floor very near to the main temple. Devotees often go to the nearby mountain which has an Idol of Goddess Saraswati on the top of the rock. The image of Lakshmi stands besides the Goddess Saraswati in the sanctum sanctorum. Due to the presence of Saraswati, Lakshmi and Kali, Basara is considered as the abode of the divine trinity.

Transport

The temple is located about 210 kilometers (via road) from the nearest city Hyderabad. It is well connected by district buses, run by TSRTC. MSRTC buses also run from Hyderabad, Nanded, etc. The nearest railway station to the temple is Basar Railway Station, located about 2.4 km away.

Trains that go to Basar Railway station:

Number	Train	Type
51433	NZB-PVR	PASSENGER
17640	AK-KCG INTER CITY	MAIL EXPRESS
17058	DEVAGIRI	MAIL EXPRESS
18310	NED-SBP NAGAWALI	BI-WEEK
57562	MMR-KCG	PASSENGER
57593	NED	PASSENGER
17232	NSL-NS	MAIL EXPRESS
57558	NZB	PASSENGER
16004	NSL-MAS WKLY	EXPRESS
17064	AJANTA MAIL	EXPRESS

LAKSHMI NARASIMHA TEMPLE, YADADRI

Sri Lakshmi Narasimha Temple also known as Yadadri and Yadagirigutta temple, is a Hindu temple situated on a hillock in Yadagirigutta of Yadadri Bhuvanagiri district of the Indian state of Telangana. The temple is an abode of Narasimha, an incarnation of Lord Vishnu. It is located about 120 kilometres (75 mi) from Suryapet and 88 kilometres (55 mi) from Nalgonda and 62 km from Hyderabad.

History

Yadagiri is named after a sage named Yadava who performed services Lord Vishnu as Narasimha. Being please with him the lord gave him darshan in three forms: jwaalaa Narasimha, ganDabhErunDa Naarasimha and yogaananda

Narasimha. Yadava begged Narasimha to remain on the hill in these forms. For this reason, the Lakshmi-Narasimhadeva temple on the hilltop has deities of Narasimha in all three forms embedded in stone in the main cave.

Deity

The temple is in a cave about 12 feet high by 30 feet long, located in back of the temple hall, by the rear pillar. You take a stairway down into the chamber and then toward the back. Jwala Narasimha is in the shape of serpent, while Yogananda Narasimha appears sitting in meditation in yoga pose. You will also see silver deities of Lakshmi-Narasimha, which are quite striking in appearance and lends presence of seeing them. To the right of the temple main door is a Hanuman temple. You'll see a long horizontal gap in the rock just below Hanuman. This is said to be where Gandabheranda Narasimha manifested. This is a very popular temple. It is said that any wish of sincere devotee visiting this temple will be fulfilled. The sanctum sanctorum or Garbhagriha is located in a cave, under a huge slating rock, which covers half the abode.

New Yadadri Temple

A new temple is being built at the old temple site. The temple was renamed as *Yadadri* by Vaishnavaite ascetic Chinna Jeeyar Swamy, who is overseeing and guiding every aspect of the new temple. For use until the new temple is completed, a temporary temple, Balalayam, was built. The main temple was to open in August 2018, and the entire temple project is expected to be completed by the end of 2019.

Renovations

The Chief Minister of Telangana, K. Chandrashekhar Rao initiated the renovation of the temple, and approved a final layout. Major renovation of the temple is being taken up with a budget of 1800 crores. The work started in 2016 and is being executed by Yadadri Temple Development Authority (YTDA). The temple owned 39 kilos of gold and 1,753 tonnes of silver for lining the gopurams and walls in the temple. The centuries-old practice of using lime mortar to join different stone parts is being used. The YTDA acquired around 1900 acres by spending 300 crores.

Sections

The sections of the temple includethe main temple, Mukha Mandapam, seven gopurams (domes) with wooden rooves, vratha peetham, Swamy Vari Udyana Vanam, kalyana mandapam, satram etc. The pillars of 12 Alvars (*those immersed in God*) in the main temple is a significant feature.

The temple entrance arch will depict Mahâbhûta (the five elements).

Temple architecture

The architecture of the temple is based on Agama Shashtra. The temple is built entirely in stone, no temple was build in stone in last 2000 years. The temple was earlier built on 2 acres. After demolishing all structures on the temple hillock, the base for the temple is now 14 acres.

Design

The project architect is Anand Sai, chosen for his understanding of the ancient designs based on silpa and Agama principles. The entire temple is built in stone. The stone designs in Yadadri were provided by the chief sthapathi of the temple, Soundara Rajan of Srirangam, Tamil Nadu.

Sculptures

Three types are stones are being used for the temple like *Krishna Sila* (Purusha Sila) for presiding deities in the sanctum sanctorum; *Sthri Sila* for deities of Goddesses; and *Napusaka Sila* for flooring and walls etc. Black granite stone is also used, based on the temple architecture of the Kakatiya Dynasty in Telangana. The black granite stone has tiny pores, that becomes strong and hard when milk, curd, oil and other liquids get into pores, according to shilipis (sculpture experts).

There are around 500 sculptors belonging to different groups like D. Hari Prasad, D Ravinder, Balasubrahmanyam, Venkatareddy, Potuluraiah and Shaikh Rabbani hailing from Tamil Nadu, Andhra Pradesh and other regions are working on the project.

Transport

Yadagirigutta is about 60 km (approx. 38 miles) from Hyderabad and is well connected by both rail and road. The nearest railway station is Raigiri (about 3 km) for passenger trains. After alighting at Raigiri, one can take an auto rickshaw or tanga.

The Hyderabad MMTS - Phase II is planned, to be extended from Ghatkesar to Raigir station, which is 5 km from Yadagirigutta.

A new bus stand is built on a 15 acres, as a part of new temple development.

RAMAPPA TEMPLE

Ramappa Temple also known as the Ramalingeswara temple, is located 77 km from Warangal, the ancient capital of the Kakatiya dynasty, 157 km from Hyderabad in the state of Telangana in southern India. It lies in a valley at Palampet village of Venkatapur Mandal, in erstwhile Mulug Taluq of Jayashankar Bhupalpally district, a tiny village long past its days of glory in the 13th and 14th centuries. An inscription in the temple dates it to the year 1213 AD and says it was built by a General Recherla Rudra, during the period of the Kakatiya ruler Ganapati Deva.

The temple is a Shivalaya, where Lord Ramalingeswara is worshipped. It stands majestically on a 6 ft high star-shaped platform. The hall in front of the sanctum has numerous carved pillars that have been positioned to create an effect that combines light and space wonderfully. The temple is named after the sculptor Ramappa, who built it, and is perhaps the only temple in India to be named after a craftsman who built it. History says that it took 40 years to build this temple.

The main structure is in a reddish sandstone, but the columns round the outside have large brackets of black basalt. These are carved as mythical animals or female dancers or musicians, and are "the masterpieces of Kakatiya art, notable for their delicate carving, sensuous postures and elongated bodies and heads".

Description

The roof (garbhalayam) of the temple is built with bricks, which are so light that they are able to float on water.

There are two small Shiva shrines on either side of the main temple. The enormous Nandi within, facing the shrine of Shiva, remains in good condition.

Nataraja Ramakrishna revived Perini Shivatandavam (Perini Dance), by seeing the sculptures in this temple. The dance poses, written in Nritta Rathnavalid by Jayapa Senaani, also appear in these sculptures.

The temple remained intact even after repeated wars, plunder and destruction during wars and natural disasters. There was a major earthquake during the 17th century which caused some damage.

Many of the smaller structures were neglected and are in ruins. The Archaeological Survey of India has taken charge of it. The main entrance gate in the outer wall of the temple is ruined.

Location

Ramappa temple is located in Palampet, Venkatapur mandal which is 19 km far from Mulugu Mandal (around 70 km off Warangal Town). It is 6 km away from Kota Gullu where another Shiva temple is located. Tourists from Hyderabad can reach to Ramappa Temple via Hanamkonda.

SRI RAJA RAJESHWARA TEMPLE

Sri Raja Rajeshwara Kshetram (holy place) is one of the most famous Hindu temples in Telangana, dedicated to Lord Shiva. It is located in the town of Vemulawada, Telangana, India.

Temple

This temple of Lord [Shiva] in the form of Raja Rajeshwara Swami is very famous in this part of the region. The presiding deity of the temple is Sri Raja Rajeswara Swamy who is locally popular as Rajanna who is adorned on both the sides by the idol of Sri Raja Rajeswari Devi on the right side and to the left is the idol of Sri Laxmi Sahitha Siddi Vinayaka.

Vemulawada Raja rajeswara temple is situated 38 km from Karimnagar. This famous temple dedicated to Lord Rajarajeswara Swamy, draws pilgrims in large numbers. There is a Dargah inside the temple complex where all devotees offer prayers, irrespective of caste and creed.

Pilgrims have divine bath in a holy tank called *Dharma Gundam*, before proceeding for darshan and these holy waters are believed to have medicinal properties. Every year at the time of Maha Shiva Rathri, devotees in large numbers flock to Vemulawada, to offer prayers to Lord Shiva. This temple also has a very special offering made by devotees called' *Koda Mokku'*. Koda mokku is a ritual where the devotee makes the pradakshinam of the temple with a kode (bull) which is vahanam(nandi) of Lord Shiva. Rajarajeshvara temple was built by King Rajaraja Chola. Inside is a massive shiva linga.

THOUSAND PILLAR TEMPLE

The Thousand Pillar Temple or Rudreshwara Swamy Temple is a historic Hindu temple located in the town of Hanamakonda, Telangana State, India. It is dedicated to Lord Shiva, Vishnu and Surya. Thousand Pillar Temple, along with "*warangal Fort*" and "*Ramappa Temple*" are added to the tentative list of World Heritage sitesrecognised by UNESCO.

History

Many Hindu temples were developed under the patronage of Ganapati Deva, Rudrama Devi and Prataparudra who were of Kakatiya dynasty. The Thousand Pillar Temple was believed to be constructed during the period between 1175–1324 CE by order of the king, Rudra Deva. It stands out to be a masterpiece and achieved major heights in terms of architectural skills by the ancient Kakatiya vishwakarma sthapathis.

It was desecrated by the Tughlaq dynasty during their invasion of the Deccan. But the Nizam of Hyderabad Mir Osman Ali Khandonated 1 Lakh INR towards this temple.

Architecture

The Thousand Pillar Temple with its ruins lies near the Hanamkonda-Warangal Highway in Telangana State, about 150 kilometres (93 mi) from the city of Hyderabad.

Rudreswara Temple locally known as Veyisthambala Gudi (Thousand pillars temple) is one of the fine and earliest available examples of Kakatiya art, architecture and sculpture. It was built by Rudra Deva, and named after him as 'Sri Rudreswara swamy temple with the presiding deity as Rudreswara, in 1163 AD in the style of later Chalukyan and early Kakatiyan Architecture, star shaped and triple shrined (Trikutalaya).

The temple is a fine specimen of architecture and sculpture with One thousand pillars.

There are richly carved pillars, perforated screens, exquisite icons; rock cut elephants and the monolithic dolerite Nandi as components of the temple. Strengthening of foundations like sand box technique, the skill of Kakatiya sculptors is manifest in adroit craftsmanship and flawless ivory carving technique in their art. The ingenuity of Kakatiya sculptors is visible in likes of lathe turned, and shiny polish in dolerite and granite stone sculpture and craft work of Nava rangamandapa.

The temple was renovated in 2004 by the Government of India. Archaeological Survey of Indiaand modern engineers have been working for the temple's further renovation.now it is located in hanamkonda

Transport

The nearest railway station is Warangal railway station,

which is 6 kilometres (3.7 miles) away from the temple. Rajiv Gandhi International Airport is the nearest airport to this temple.

MAKKAH MASJID, HYDERABAD

Mecca Masjid, is one of the oldest mosques in Hyderabad, Telangana in India, and it is one of the largest masjids in India. Makkah Masjid is a listed heritage building in the old city of Hyderabad, close to the historic landmarks of Chowmahalla Palace, Laad Bazaar, and Charminar.

Muhammad Quli Qutb Shah, the fifth ruler of the Qutb Shahi dynasty, commissioned bricks to be made from the soil brought from Mecca, the holiest site of Islam, and used them in the construction of the central arch of the mosque, thus giving the mosque its name. It formed the centerpiece around which the city was planned by Muhammad Quli Qutub Shah.

History and construction

Makkah Masjid was built during the reign of Muhammad Quli Qutb Shah, the 5th Qutb Shahi Sultan of Golconda (now Hyderabad). The three arched facades have been carved from a single piece of granite, which took five years to quarry. More than 8,000 workers were employed to build the mosque. Muhammad Quli Qutb Shah personally laid the foundation stone and constructed it.

Jean-Baptiste Tavernier, the French explorer, in his travelogue observed;

"It is about 50 years since they began to build a splendid pagoda in the town which will be the grandest in all India when it is completed. The size of the stone is the subject of special accomplishment, and that of a niche, which is its place for prayer, is an entire rock of such enormous size that they spent five years in quarrying it, and 500 to 600 men were employed continually on its work. It required still more time to roll it up on to conveyance by which they brought it to the pagoda; and they took 1400 oxen to draw it."

Architecture and design

The main hall of the mosque is 75 feet high, 220 feet wide and 180 feet long, enough to accommodate 10,000 worshipers at a time. Fifteen arches support the roof of the main hall, five on each of the three sides. A wall rises on the fourth side to provide Mihrab.

At the peak of the minarets flanking the mosque is an arched gallery, and above that a smallish dome and a spire. Inscriptions from the Qur'an adorn many of the arches and doors. The main structure of the mosque is sandwiched between two massive octagonal columns made out of a single piece of granite. The cornices running around the entire mosque structure and the floral motifs and friezes over the arches remind the tourist of the great attention paid to detail in Qutub Shahi architecture. They have a close resemblance to the arches at Charminar and Golkonda Fort.

On the four sides of the roof on the main mosque, the ramparts are made of granite planks in the shape of inverted conches perched on pedestals. From the cornice of the mosque, its minarets are not as high as the minarets on the mazaar (Nizams tombs) haven from their cornice. The octagonal columns have arched balconies on level with the roof of the mosque with an awning for a canopy, above which the column continues upwards till it is crowned by a dome and spire.

Tombs

The entrance courtyard it is best of the mosque, a rectangular, arched and canopied building houses the marble graves ofrulers of the Asaf Jahi dynasty rulers. This structure came up during the rule of the Asaf Jah rulers. It contains the tombs of the Asaf Jahi rulers except the *1st*and the *last Nizam* - Mir Osman Ali Khan-who is buried in Judi Mosque opposite King Kothi Palace

At both ends of this resting place for the Asaf Jahi's and very much a part of it, are two rectangular blocks with four minarets each. These minarets have elegant and circular balconies with low ornamental walls and arches. Above them is an octagonal inverted platter from which the rest of the minaret soars till it is arrested by a dome and a spire.

Maintenance issue

The Makkah Masjid is a listed heritage building, however, lack of maintenance and growing pollution has withered and cracked the structure. It only received a chemical wash in 1995.

Legends

On the edge of the pond are two stone and slab benches, whoever sits on them, according to legend, returns to sit on them

A room in the courtyard is believed to house a hair of the Islamic prophet Muhammed.

Bombing

On 18 May 2007, a bomb exploded inside the Makkah Masjid at the time of Friday prayers, killing at least thirteen people and injuring dozens.

KHAIRTABAD MOSQUE

Khairtabad Mosque is in Khairatabad. Today Khairtabad is a well-known locality built around the mosque. The area had become a major business and IT hub of Hyderabad, India.

History

Khairtabad Mosque was built by Khairunisa Begum in 1626 AD, also known as Ma Saheba, daughter of VI Sultan Muhammad Qutb Shah(1612–1626 AD). She built the mosque for her tutor Akhund Mulla Abul Malik.

There is an empty domed building adjacent to the mosque. The reason for its being devoid of any grave is that it was built by Akhund for self burial; as he died during his pilgrimage to Haj in Mecca, the dome remains vacant.

Khairunisa Begum asked his son-in-law Hussain Shah Wali to construct a palace, a mosque and a tank for the princess. The tank later became famous as Hussain Sagar, built in the northern boundary of Khairtabad.

Architecture

Khairatabad Mosque was designed and constructed by Hussain Shah Wali. The mosque has a three-arch opening in front. The slender minarets of the mosque have lot of decorative work and the Jali (net) work is worth seeing. The architecture of the mosque presents perfect harmony from bottom to top. The chief praying hall is on a raised platform.

INTACH AP, India had declared it as a heritage site.

Negligence

An article in *The Hindu*, "Crying for Attention," cited plant growth invading local mosques. "It doesn't require a connoisseur to see the rot that has set in the Qutb Shahi Khairtabad Mosque and Khairati Begum's tomb in Khairatabad," both protected architectural monuments. "The lime plaster and stuccowork can be seen peeling off at many places. There are ... fissures in the structure with vegetation growing from the minarets. The vegetal growth is particularly heavy at the rear of the mosque."

Restoration

The Department of Archaeology and Museums has decided to take up repair work in the mosque and earmarked a sum of Rs. 25 lakhs under the plan budget. "The work has been awarded and it will commence soon," said J. Kedeshwari, director, Archaeology and Museums.

For the first time the department plans to take up conservation and restoration of the Premavati mosque and the Hakimpet Sarai at a cost of Rs. 5 crores. It's been delayed by a lack of budgetary and technical support, say officials.

TOLI MASJID

Toli Masjid (1671 AD), also known as Damri Masjid, is a mosque in Karwan, Hyderabad, India. It is 2 km from the Golconda fort on the way to Charminar. Built by Mir Musa Khan Mahaldar during the reign of Abdullah Qutb Shah in (1082 AH). This mosque is INTACH awarded and a declared heritage site by Archaeological Survey of India. On scale of architecture Toli Mosque ranks next after Mecca Masjid, Hyderabad, India.

History

Built by Mir Musa Khan Mahaldar in 1671 AD during the rule of Sultan Abdullah Qutub Shah, it is one of the finest examples of Qutub Shahi architecture. He used architect Mecca Masjid of Hyderabad and royal architect of Sultan Abdullah Qutub Shah.

There is a chapter in the royal records called the "Gulzar-e-Asafia." It mentions that when the royal architect was building Mecca Masjid, he was given one damri/damdi (coin) out of every rupee spent on it. The sum of money thus collected was used by Musa Khan to construct the Toli Masjid. Hence, this masjid is also called Damri Masjid.

Architecture

The mosque is built on a raised platform with a high plinth, divided into two halls, the outer one having five-arched openings, among five outer arches the central arch is slightly wider and more ornate. Two minarets of 20 metres each flank the edifice. The parapets on top comprise a series of miniature arches with perforated screens of different designs. There are five beautiful arches each with lotus medallions in the spandrels. The central arch is a bit wider and more ornate than the remaining four.

The inscription in the prayer hall reveals that Musa Khan (who played an important role in the accession of the last Qutb Shahi Sultan, Abul Hasan Qutb Shah to the throne of Golconda) built the mosque. The Musa Burj (bastion) of the Golconda fort is also his work.

The upper half of this mosque is the most beautifully decorated. The parapet consists of a series of arched jali screens, each of a different pattern. Above this runs a row of tiny notches punctuated by six finials. The elaborately decorated minarets have three receding tiers of octagonal galleries, the central one raised on a series of deeply recessed, carved moldings and petals. The minaret shaft is covered with rounded patterns. This composition is adorned by a circular dome and a brass finial.

Deterioration

According to *The Hindu*, the land around the Toli Masjid had been encroached by the local residents under political influence, and due to pollution and lack of maintenance the mosque minarets are losing its carved beauty.

MAJOR TOURIST DESTINATIONS

City Tours

Hyderabad and Warangal are the largest cities with many tourist places.

Monuments

Charminar, Golconda Fort, Qutb Shahi Tombs, Chowmahalla Palace, Falaknuma Palace and Bhongir Fort, are some of the monuments in the state.

- Charminar, built in 1591 CE, is a monument and mosque located in Hyderabad, Telangana, India. The landmark has become a global icon of Hyderabad, listed among the most recognized structures of India. The Charminar is on the east bank of Musi river. To the northeast lies the Laad Bazaar and in the west end lies the granite-made richly ornamented Makkah Masjid. The English name is a transliteration and combination of the Urdu words Châr and Minar, translating to "Four Towers"; the eponymous towers are ornate minarets attached and supported by four grand arches.
- Golconda Fort – Once abandoned by Qutub Shahis,

Golconda Fort is one of the most magnificent fortress complexes in India. Seated on a hill on one side and spiraling fort on the other, its location and internal design made it one of the strongest forts in India.

Kakatiya Kala Thoranam

- Qutb Shahi Tombs – Home to various Tombs dedicated to Rulers of Qutub Shahi dynasty, located at Shaikpet, near Golconda Fort. These are an example of Deccan architecture with large minarets, huge domes, delicate marble designs and multiple inner passages.
- Kakatiya Kala Thoranam:It is a historical arch and symbol of the Kakatiya Dynasty in Warangal district. The arch was built around 1200 CE during the rule of Kakatiya dynasty. It is a huge stone sculpture created as a *Kirti*

Thoranam, meaning The Glory Arch.A depiction of the arch forms the main symbol in the Emblem of Telangana for the state of Telangana.

- Bhongir Fort:It is a Fort located in Bhongir, Nalgonda district, India. It was built in the 10th century on an isolated monolithic rock by the Western Chalukya ruler Tribhuvanamalla Vikramaditya VI and was thus named after him as Tribhuvanagiri.At the foot of the fortified rocks 609.6 meters above the sea level stands the town of Bhongir, it has a unique egg-shaped construction with two entry points protected by huge rocks, so the fort was considered practically impregnable by invading armies. The fort is associated with the rule of queen Rudramadevi and her grandson Prataparudra II.
- Paigah Tombs – These are recently discovered series of mausoleums with unique geometrical sculptures which were no where found in the world. These are located at Chandrayanagutta. Paigahs were noblemen under the reign of Nizams.Paigah Mosque Spanish Mosque, Begumpet : This Mosque is one of the marvelous mosques present in Secunderabad/Hyderabad. It's well known among the people because of its amazing architecture. The architecture followed in this mosque is the Andalusi/ Spanish Architecture. The mosque was constructed by Sir Vicar-ul-Umra a Paigah Nawab in 1906.

Religious Tourism

- Kulpakji or Kolanupaka Temple: Kulpakji is a 2,000 years old Jain Temple at the village of Kolanupaka in Nalgonda district. This temple is one of the oldest temple in South India and considered famous for state of the art architecture and sculptures. The image of Lord Rishabhanatha, carved of a green stone has been historically famous as "Manikyaswami" and The 130 centimetres (51 in) statue of Lord Mahaveer is made of a single piece of jade. It is said the Manikyasami image of Rishabhantha was originally worshipped by Mandodari, the wife of Ravana and it was brought here by the ruler Sankar of Kalyana The interior of the temple is made by red sand stone and white marble.

Kulpakji

- Yadagirigutta: Lord Vishnu (whose reincarnation is Lord Narasimha). The main deity is Lakshmi Narasimha Swamy.Located in Nalgonda District. In Ancient days Sri Yada Maharshi son of Sri Rushyashrunga Maharshi with the Blessings of Anjaneya Swamy had performed great penance for Lord Narasimha Swamy. After securing blessing for his penance Lord Narasimha had come into existence in Five Avatharas called as Sri Jwala Narasimha, Sri Yogananda Narasimha, Sri Ugra Narasimha, Sri Gandaberunda Narasimha, Sri Lakshmi Narasimha. As such this is known as "Pancha Narasimha Kshetram"
- Thousand Pillar Temple is one of the oldest temples of South India that was built by the kakatiya. It is believed that the Thousand Pillar Temple was built by King Rudra

Deva in 1163 AD. The Thousand Pillar Temple is a specimen of the Kakatiyan style of architecture of the 12th century. There are one thousand pillars in the building and the temple, but no pillar obstructs a person in any point of the temple to see the god in the other temple.

- Bhadrachalam Temple is a temple to Lord Rama in the town of Bhadrachalam in Khammam district. It is situated on the banks of the river Godavari. This is the place where Kancherla Gopanna (1620–1680) wrote his devotional songs dedicated to Lord Rama. Sri Rama Navami, a celebration of the Marriage of Lord Rama and Sita, is celebrated here every year. Government of Telangana sends pearls for the event.
- Sri Raja Rajeshwara temple, Vemulawada is a site of pilgrimage for both Hindu (particularly devotees of Vishnu and Shiva) and Muslim worshippers. Built by Chalukya Kings between AD 750 and 975, the complex is named for its presiding deity Sri Raja Rajeswara Swamy, an incarnation of Lord Shiva. It houses several temples dedicated to other deities including Sri Rama, Lakshmana, Lakshmi, Ganapathy, Lord Padmanabha Swamy and Lord Bhimeshwara.This Shrine is popularly known as 'Dakshina Kasi' [Southern Banaras] and also as "Harihara Kshetram" for their being two Vaisnava Temples in main Temple complex i.e., Sri Anantha Padmanabha Swamy Temple & Sri Seetharama Chandra Swamy Temple The complex also contains a 400-year-old mosque which stands as an ample evidence for religious tolerance .The temple is located in Karimnagar District.
- Ramappa Temple: An inscription in the temple dates it to the year 1213 and said to have been built by a General Recherla Rudra, during the period of the Kakatiya ruler Ganapati Deva.
- Birla Mandir, Hyderabad: Built on a 280 feet (85 m) high hillock called Naubath Pahad on a 13 acres (53,000 m2) plot in Hyderabad

- Basara: Gnana Saraswati Temple (Goddess of Knowledge) is located on the banks of the river Godavari in Adilabad District
- Nelakondapalli:NelakondapallIis famous for Birthplace of Bhakta Ramadasu (Sri Ramadas) who built the Sita Ramachandraswamy temple at Bhadrachalam, Nelakondapally is famous for 'Budha Stupa', South India's biggest budha stupha located at Nelakondaplly, It is Shariraka stupa (built on body part of Lord Bhudha)in 3rd century B.C.

Mecca Masjid frontage

- Mecca Masjid, is one of the oldest mosques in Hyderabad, Telangana in India, And it is one of the largest Mosques in India. Makkah Masjid is a listed heritage building in the old city of Hyderabad, close to the historic landmarks of Chowmahalla Palace, Laad Bazaar, and Charminar. Muhammad Quli Qutb Shah, the fifth ruler of the Qutb Shahi dynasty, commissioned bricks to be made from the soil brought from Mecca, the holiest site of Islam, and used them in the construction of the central arch of the mosque, thus giving the mosque its name. It formed the centerpiece around which the city was planned by Muhammad Quli Qutub Shah.

The Church of South IndiaCathedral at Medak, one of the largest churches in Asia

- Medak Church at Medak in Telangana, India, is the largest church in Telangana and has been the cathedral church of the Diocese of Medak of the Church of South India since 1947. Originally built by British Wesleyan Methodists, it was consecrated on 25 December 1924. The Medak diocese is the single largest diocese in Asia and the second in the world after the Vatican. The church was built under the stewardship of the Methodist Christian, the Reverend Charles Walker Posnett, who was driven by the motto *My best for my Lord.* Charles Posnett had arrived in Secunderabad in 1895, and after first ministering among British soldiers at Trimullghery, had launched into the villages and had reached Medak village in 1896.
- Kuchadri sri venkateshwara swamy temple an ancient Hindu temple in Kuchanpally, Medak District

- Other religious places include the Buddhist centres at Nelakondapalli, Dhulikatta Phanigiri and Kolanpaka.

Water falls

- Kuntala Waterfall, located in Kuntala, Adilabad district, at 45 metres (148 ft), is the biggest in the state. There are other interesting waterfalls in Telangana state.
- Mallela Theertham, at a distance of 58 km from Srisailam & 173 km from Hyderabad is a charming waterfall located in the dense Nallamala Forest. This is one of the popular tourist attractions to visit around Hyderabad.
- Bheemuni Paadam Waterfalls: At a distance of 10 km from Gudur Bus Stand, 51 km from Warangal, 88 km from Khammam Bus Station and 200 km from Hyderabad, Bheemuni Paadam Waterfalls is a picturesque waterfall located at Gudur in Warangal District of Telangana.
- Pochera Falls (Near Kuntala Falls) - At a distance of 40 km from Nirmal, 50 km from Adilabad, 257 km from Hyderabad and 22 km from Kuntala Falls, Pochera Falls is a pretty waterfall on Kadam River. The falls are located at a distance of 10 km from Neredikonda village between Nirmal & Adilabad (a diversion is required at Boath cross roads)
- Gayatri Waterfalls- At a distance of 5 km from Tarnam Khurd Village, 19 km from Kuntala Waterfalls, 38 km from Nirmal, 59 km Adilabad and 270 km from Hyderabad, Gayathri Waterfalls is a beautiful place located in Adilabad district of Telangana.

'*sabetham* water fall in sabetham near godavarikani of 15 km and in ramagundam mandal in karimnagar beautiful location with forest of green hills

8

Population and Religion

DEMOGRAPHICS

Religion in Telangana

Religion	Percent
Hinduism	85.09%
Islam	12.68%
Christianity	1.3%
Others	0.9%

According to the Backward Regions Grant Fund Programme 2009–10, there are 9 backward districts (all except Hyderabad) from Telangana and the rest are from other regions.

The religious makeup of Telangana is about 85.1% Hindu, 12.7% Muslim, and 1.3% Christian, and 0.9% others.

Telugu is the official language of Telangana and Urdu is the second official language of the state. About 77% of the population of Telangana speak Telugu, 12% speak Urdu, and 13% speak other languages. Before 1948, Urdu was the official language of Hyderabad State, and due to a lack of Telugu-language educational institutions, Urdu was the language of the educated elite of Telangana. After 1948, once Hyderabad State joined the new Republic of India, Telugu became the language of government, and as Telugu was introduced as the medium of instruction in schools and colleges, the use of Urdu among non Hyderabadi Muslims decreased. Both Telugu and Urdu are used in services across the state, such as the Telangana Legislature website, with Telugu and Urdu versions of the website available, as well as the Hyderabad Metro, wherein both languages are used on station names and signs along with English and Hindi. The Urdu spoken in Telangana is called Hyderabadi Urdu, which in itself is a dialect of the larger Dakhini Urdu dialects of South India. Although the language is orally spoken by most Hyderabadi Muslims, the language in a literary context has long been lost, and standard Urdu is used.

According to the 2011 census, Telangana's literacy rate is 66.46%. Male literacy and female literacy are 74.95% and 57.92%, respectively. Hyderabad district leading with 80.96% and Mahabubnagar district at the bottom with 56.06%.

RELIGION

The major religions of the people are Hinduism and Islam, though Buddhism was the dominant religion up to the 6th century. It is the home of Mahayana Buddhism as revealed by the monuments of Nagarjunakonda. Acharaya Nagarjuna presided over the World University at Sri Parvata. Hinduism was revived during the time of the Chalukyas and the Kakatiyas in the 12th century. The Vijayanagar rule saw the glorious days of Hinduism when the famed emperors, Krishnadeva Raya in particular, built new temples and beautified the old ones. Siva, Vishnu, Hanuman and Ganapati have been the popular Hindu Gods. The Vugra Narasimha Swami Temple at Yadagirigutta and Thousand Pillar Temple at Warangal are among the oldest shrines in the state attracting people from different parts of the country for hundreds of years.

In terms of influence, Islam occupies the second place. It started spreading from the 14th century onwards. Mosques began to come up in many parts of the region during the Muslim rule. Christianity began to spread from 1701, Especially among the socially disabled people. Educational institutions and churches grew in number in the Circars in the 18th-19th centuries when the East India Company and later the British government encouraged them. Other European countries were also active in building churches and taking care of the weaker sections of the people.

Pilgrimages in Telangana

Bhadrachalam Temple

Yadadri : Lord Vishnu (whose reincarnation is Lord Narasimha). The main deity is Lakshmi Narasimha Swamy. Located in Yadadri District. In Ancient days Sri Yada Maharshi son of Sri Rushyashrunga Maharshi with the Blessings of Anjaneya Swamy had performed great penance for Lord Narasimha Swamy. After securing blessing for his penance Lord Narasimha had come into existence in Five Avatharas called as Sri Jwala Narasimha, Sri Yogananda Narasimha, Sri Ugra Narasimha, Sri Gandaberunda Narasimha, Sri Lakshmi Narasimha. As such this is known

Bhadrachalam Temple is a Lord Sree Sita Ramachandra Swamy Temple in Bhadrachalam, Bhadradri District. Bhadrachalam-The name derived from Bhadragiri (Mountain of Bhadra-a boon child of Meru and Menaka). According to an

Ithihasas, the significance of this shrine dates back to the Ramayana Era. This coherent hill place existed in "Dandakaranya" Of Ramayanaperiod where Rama with his consort Sita and brother Laxmana had spent their vanavasa-and Parnashaala(the place connected to the famous Golden Deer and the place from where Sita was abducted by Ravana.) is also in the vicinity of this temple site. It is at this Mandir site that, long after Ramavatara, Bhagawan Mahavishnu manifested Himself as Rama again to fulfil a promise He made to His Bhakta Bhadra, who continued his Tapas through Yugas, praying for the grace of the Bhagawan Sri Ramachandra murthy.

Jamalapuram Temple is a Lord Sree Venkateswara Swamy Temple in Jamalapuram, near Errupalem, Khammam District is a famous temple in Khammam district of Telangana and is famously known as Telangana Tirupathi. The presiding deity in this temple is Lord Balaji and is said to be a swayambhu Lord, who self-manifested in this place. Since it is a swayambhoo temple, this temple seems to have been in existence from thousands of years. It was renovated by Sri Krishna Devarayalu, the emperor of Vijayanagara kingdom. The temple is located in a serene pleasant ambience surrounded by lush green hills. The temple has sub-shrines for Padmavathi Ammavaru, Sri Alivelu Ammavaru, Lord Shiva, Lord Ganesh, Lord Ayyappa, and Lord Anjaneya.

Sri Raja Rajeshwara temple, Vemulawada is a site of pilgrimage for both Hindu (particularly devotees of Vishnu and Shiva) and Muslim worshippers. Built by Chalukya Kings between AD 750 and 975, the complex is named for its presiding deity Sri Raja Rajeswara Swamy, an incarnation of Lord Shiva. It houses several temples dedicated to other deities including Sri Rama, Lakshmana, Lakshmi, Ganapathy, Lord Padmanabha Swamy and Lord Bhimeshwara.This Shrine is popularly known as 'Dakshina Kasi' [Southern Banaras] and also as "Harihara Kshetram" for their being two Vaisnava Temples in main Temple complex i.e., Sri Anantha Padmanabha Swamy Temple & Sri Seetharama Chandra Swamy Temple The complex also contains a 400-year-old mosque which stands as an ample evidence for religious tolerance .The temple is located in Karimnagar District.

Birla Mandir, Hyderabad: Built on a 280 feet (85 m) high hillock called Naubath Pahad on a 13 acres (53,000 m2) plot in Hyderabad

Basara: Gnana Saraswati Temple (Goddess of Knowledge) is located on the Deccan platue

Mecca Masjid, is one of the oldest mosques in Hyderabad, Telangana in India, And it is one of the largest Mosques in India. Makkah Masjid is a listed heritage building in the old city of Hyderabad, close to the historic landmarks of Chowmahalla Palace, Laad Bazaar, and Charminar. Muhammad Quli Qutb Shah, the fifth ruler of the Qutb Shahi dynasty, commissioned bricks to be made from the soil brought from Mecca, the holiest site of Islam, and used them in the construction of the central arch of the mosque, thus giving the mosque its name. It formed the centerpiece around which the city was planned by Muhammad Quli Qutub Shah.

Medak Church at Medak in Telangana, India, is the largest church in Telangana and has been the cathedral church of the Diocese of Medak of the Church of South India since 1947. Originally built by British Wesleyan Methodists, it was consecrated on 25 December 1924. The Medak diocese is the single largest diocese in Asia and the second in the world after the Vatican. The church was built under the stewardship of the Methodist Christian, the Reverend Charles Walker Posnett, who was driven by the motto *My best for my Lord.* Charles Posnett had arrived in Secunderabad in 1895, and after first ministering among British soldiers at Trimullghery, had launched into the villages and had reached Medak village in 1896.

Banjara (Lambadi) spiritual / religious persons

Jairam Bapuji, Sevya Bapuji are the very famous Banjara Or Lambadi Spiritual Persons from Balu Thanda / Jairam Thanda, Madgul Mandal, Mahabubnagar District,Telangana.

9

Art, Architecture, Fair and Festivals

ART AND CULTURE OF TELANGANA

Telangana is a storehouse of creativity which is prevalent in its collection of art and craft. Developed in the 16th century, the Golconda style is an old method of blending foreign techniques. A dash of bright gold and white colour is used in the Golconda style. The Hyderabad style emerged in the 17th century under the influence of Nizams.

Dhokra or Dokra is a famous craft which is also known as Bell Metalcraft. Here artisans produce figurines, peacocks, elephants, horses, tribal gods and other variety of birds and animals which are made of brass. It originated in West Bengal, Chhatisgarh and Jharkhand.

Bidri craft is said to have brought in by migrants. It is an art where silver is engraved on metal. The name is derived from a town called Bidar (now in Karnataka). Beautiful jewellery boxes, hukka, buttons and other things are made using this art.

Religion of Telangana

Telangana is home to diverse culture and religions. Till 6th century, the region was predominantly ruled by the Buddhist and is the home of Mahayana Buddhism. From the 14th century onwards Islam began to spread. Urdu is the second widely spoken language in the state. Christianity began to spread from 1701 and later, East India Company and British Raaj encouraged more of Christian culture. Hinduism was rekindled in the 12th century. Emperors like Krishnadeva Ray, in particular, built temples and embellished the old ones.

Festivals of Telangana

With so many religion it is expected to host some festivals as well. To start with, Bathukamma is a part of Dasara festivities which is unique to Telangana. Celebrated by Hindu women, this festival falls in September?October and as per the lunar calendar. In Telugu, 'Bathukamma' meaning 'Mother Goddess Come Alive', is worshipped in the form of Bathukamma, the goddess of womanhood - Maha Gauri Devi.

Bonalu is another Hindu Festival, celebrated during June/ July where Goddess Maa Kali is worshipped. The festival is considered a thanksgiving to the Goddess for fulfilling the desires of devotees. A great family feast follows after the massive offering. The meal is the meat of a goat or a chicken which is offered ceremonially to the goddess, and it is considered sacred. The offering of alcohol is also seen as a must.

Ramzan is the main festival of Muslims and Moharram too is celebrated on a large scale in Telangana. It is known as 'primarily panduga' where Pir means Master. Many Hindus also actively take part in the festival.

Cuisine of Telangana

Cuisine gets a makeover as the dishes are a direct influence on the existing culture of that place. Telangana mainly has two distinct cuisines - Telegu and Hyderabadi where former is mainly spicy in which millet, jowar, and bajra dominate. The latter, however, is said to have been developed by the Qutb Shahi dynasty and the Nizams of Hyderabad. It has fused the flavours of Persian, Mughlai, Marathwada, Telugu and Turkish cuisines with a fine mixture of aromatic spices and herbs. It has city specific specialities like Hyderabadi biryani, Aurangabad Naan Qalia, Gulbarga Tahari and Bidar Kalyani Biryani.

Dry coconut, red chillies and tamarind along with spices form the main ingredients of Hyderabadi cuisine making it stand apart from North Indian recipes. Sakinalu is a popular savoury in Telangana, which is prepared during Makara Sankranti. This a deep-fried snack made of rice flour, sesame seeds and flavoured with ajwain (carom seeds or vaamu in Telugu). These are harder and spicier than the Andhra varieties. Garijelu is a dumpling dish cooked with sweet stuffing with mutton or chicken keema. People give a lot of importance to the right temperature for cooking. Slow cooking or dum pukh is the key to turn the dishes lip smacking.

Traditional Dresses of Telangana

Telangana is famous for its weaving and dying techniques because its cotton producing units are world famous. The most common apparel worn by women is saree along with langa voni, salwar kameez and churidar. The famous sarees made in Telangana include Pochampally Saree and Gadwal saree. Bhoodan Pochampally, a Mandal in Nalgonda District, is known for its Ikat style of sarees and material. Pochampally weave is commonly called ikkat or tie and dye weave. Male clothing includes the traditional Dhoti which is also known as Pancha. The Hyderabadi Sherwani used to be the dress of choice of the Nizam of Hyderabad and Hyderabadi nobles. Sherwani is usually worn by the groom during the wedding ceremonies.

Cultural Dances of Telangana

Perini Thandavam is an ancient dance form performed by males. Legends say that warriors used to carry out this dance before the idol of Lord Siva before going to the battlefield during the reign of Kakatiyas. This classical dance uses 'Prerana' which means inspiration and is dedicated to Lord Shiva. The other widely famous dances in Telangana are Gusadi Dance, Kuchipudi, Tribal Dhimsa Dance, Lambadi Dance, etc.

Burra Katha is a form of dance which has evolved from a dance called Tandana Katha. It is mainly performed by a group of three main artists in the centre. Bhamakalpam and Gollakalapam are famous traditional dances which emphasise on the moral values initiated by Sidhenra Yogi.

Dandaria is a dance performed by the Gonds of Northern Hyderabad. The Gonds believe that they are the descendants of Pandavas. The male dancers dance with their Dandas and go from village to village to host functions.

Bonalu is the folk festival of Telangana where we see the colourfully dressed female dancers balancing pots (Bonalu), to the beats and tunes in praise of Mahankali. Male dancers called Potharajus to precede the female dancers to the temple adding colour to the festivity.

Telangana, a word to some but to its inhabitants, the name is a celebration. The state was born after a huge struggle where everyone maintained their unity with an unprecedented belief in victory. The state's culture, tradition and its uniqueness still linger in one's memory after their visit. Truly, a place worth exploring!

FESTIVALS OF TELANGANA

This tradition is just one of several unique traditions of Telangana. While the gods and goddesses of Hindu pantheon are worshipped and most of the famous Hindu festivals are celebrated in this region, here we write about some that are local to Telangana.

Sammakka Saralamma Jatara

As we mentioned earlier, this Jatara (fair) is the second largest in India after the Kumbh Mela. Held every two years at a remote village called Medaram in the Eturnagaram Wildlife Sanctuary, the fair is a tribal gathering to commemorate the fight of a mother and daughter against the reigning rulers. One of the legends mentions that Samakka was found by hunters as a baby playing among tigers. She was adopted by the head of the tribe and later married a tribal chief under the Kakatiya rulers. She fought valiantly and caused a lot of damage to the enemy after her entire family including the daughter Sarakka perished in a war with the larger, better equipped Kakatiya army. The Kakatiya Prime Minister, after seeing her bravery and valour, offers Sammakka peace and a position as the Chief Queen but she rejects the proposal to avenge her dead family. It is said that she disappeared into the forest after being severely injured in a battle and promised her people that she will look after them as long as they remembered her.

Bathukamma

Bathukamma festival indicates the beginning of Sarad or Sharath Ruthu and is celebrated by Hindu women in the months of September/October just before Dussehra. Bathukamma is a flower stack, arranged with different unique seasonal flowers most of them with medicinal values, in seven concentric layers in the shape of temple gopuram. For 9 days during the festival, women and young girls gather with their Bathukammas in an open area, sing folks songs, clap and dance around them. On the final day of the festival, women carry the Bathukammas on their heads to water bodies and immerse them there. It is believed that the flowers used in the Bathukamma have a purifying effect on the water.

Bonalu

Bonalu, is a festival that celebrates Goddess Mahakali and is considered as a thanksgiving for fulfilment of vows. Bonam means Bojanam or a Meal in Telugu, an offering to the Mother Goddess. It is said that this festival started in 1813 when a plague broke out in Hyderabad and Secunderabad. The military battalion from Hyderabad which was stationed in Ujjain, Madhya Pradesh prayed at the Mahankaal temple there for the peoples' wellbeing. After the plague ended, the battalion came back to the city and installed an idol of the goddess and every year Bonalu is celebrated to thank the goddess. The festivities are marked with devotees congregating at Mahankali temples, processions, feasts and Pothuraju (the brother of the goddess, represented by bare-bodied man, wearing a small tightly draped red dhoti, and anointed with turmeric on his body and vermilion on his forehead).

10

Education

EDUCATION IN TELANGANA

Telangana has multiple institutes of higher education universities along with numerous primary and secondary schools.

NIT Warangal main gate

Telangana has multiple institutes of higher education universities along with numerous primary and secondary schools. The state is home to a number of institutes, which impart higher education. The Department of Higher Education deals with matters relating to education at various levels in the State of Telangana.

The Government has established Rajiv Gandhi University of Knowledge Technologies Basar (RGUKT Basar) in 2008 to cater to the educational needs of the gifted rural youth of Telangana. The higher education includes many colleges, universities and research institutes providing professional education in the fields of arts, humanities, science, engineering, law, medicine, business, and veterinary sciences, with undergraduate and post-graduation.

Telangana Education

Education and health are critical social sectors which need active intervention by the government to steer human capital for economic development of the state.

Telangana government has taken up the process of overhauling and strengthening the public education system from the kindergarten level to degree education at college levels in a phased and systematic manner.

Adequate investments are being made in education to make the people contribute to the goal of 'Bangaru Telangana'.

A number of new initiatives have been taken to provide universal and compulsory education to all in order to improve their socio-economic conditions.

Hostels in Telangana

The construction of 34 integrated welfare hostel complexes (IWHCs) has been taken up for providing basic amenities and other facilities to hostellers at a cost of Rs 1.68 crore per complex which can accommodate 400 students from SC, ST and BC communities.

Ananda Nilayams

The inmates of nearly 33 Ananda Nilayams (destitute homes) who are orphans and from families engaged in unclean occupations are provided all facilities on par with the boarders in social welfare hostels.

College Hostels

At present 183 college hostels in the state with 11,391 students who are given post-matric scholarships (for both SC and backward classes) as well as full reimbursement of tuition fee.

Ambedkar Overseas Vidya Nidhi

To help scheduled caste students pursue higher education in foreign universities an assistance of Rs 10lakh each is sanctioned to meritorious students.

Residential Educational Institutions Society

Telangana Social Welfare Residential Educational Institutions Society (TSWREIS) runs 134 schools for students from Classes V to XII with English as medium of instruction. Having a structured reservation quotas, there are nearly 71,493 students enrolled in these schools.

TSWREIS has evolved as an institution that specifically cares for girls with about 88 institutions (66.16 %) reserved for girls.

TSWRIES has robust infrastructure with 121 schools having their own buildings and another 13 are under construction.

TSWREIS has leveraged new technologies both in its administration and educational curriculum and as a result all its 134 schools are part of an intranet for high-speed web connectivity.

The academic progress of the students and teachers is monitored online through a online monitoring system.

Ashram Schools and Hostels

Tribal welfare department is maintaining 283 Ashram Schools which have 85,843 ST students in all; 212 hostels in which 40,763 youths are staying and 101 post matric hostels with boarder strength of 20,100 students.

The pass percentage in SSC public exams held in March 2014 is 84.21% for ST students.

Gurukulam in Telangana

Gurukulam runs 150 institutions with a strength of 38,511 students. Nearly 88.67% of the students of tribal welfare residential schools passed in SSC public exam held in March, 2014.

The percentage of students of tribal welfare residential junior colleges passed in intermediate public exam is 85.80% against the state average of 55.85%.

Hostels for college students

To promote higher education among the backward classes, official orders have been issued for setting up one hostel each for boys and girls in each assembly constituency in Telangana.

At present, 247 college hostels are functioning (123 boys hostels and 124 girls) with a total strength of 17,334 (8,917 boys and 8,417 girls) during the year 2014-15.

All these college hostels for boys and girls have an admission pattern of 69% for backward classes, 15% SC, 6% ST and 10% minorities for encouraging social integration.

Residential Schools in Telangana

There are 19 BC residential schools (12 for boys and 7 for girls) with a total strength of 7,584 students (5,218 boys and 2,366 girls) in the state.

All these residential schools have an admission quota of 74% for backward classes, 15% SC, 6% ST, 2% economically backward classes and 3% for orphans. Kowdipally school in Medak district is exclusively meant for the children belonging to fishermen community.

Post-matric scholarships, fee reimbursement

All eligible BC students having an annual family income up to Rs 1 lakh per annum are sanctioned post matric scholarships and reimbursement of tuition fee on saturation basis.

During 2013-14, 6.96 lakh BC students were sanctioned scholarships and tuition reimbursement. The eligibility criteria for EBCs (economically backward classes) for getting reimbursement of tuition fee are the same as those applicable for BCs.

School education in Telangana

With a literacy rate of 66.46% as against national average of 72.99%, Telangana has 2 crore literates in all - 1.17 crore males and 90.35 lakh females.

Due to sustained efforts, the state has achieved 99% access at elementary level and 91.5% at secondary level by opening schools across districts as per national standards.

There are 61.78 lakh school going children for which the state has 43,208 schools under various management systems.

Close to realising the objective of universalisation of primary education, Telangana has made rapid strides in improving the physical infrastructure at primary level of school education.

As a result of all these efforts, the teacher-pupil ratio for primary, upper primary and high school categories are 27, 23 and 24 respectively for 2014-15.

With active intervention by the government, a large number of out-of-school children were brought into formal education system and the enrolment in all types of schools in 2014-15 was 60.76 lakh.

The percentage of school enrolment drops as one goes from lower classes to higher secondary classes as the dropout for Telangana is 22.32% at the primary level (Classes I to V) and 38.21 at the secondary level (up to Class X)

Intermediate Education

There are 397 junior colleges and 4 vocational junior colleges under the administrative control of the Director of Intermediate Education.

Besides, 43 privately owned junior colleges take instructions from the directorate with regard to grant-in-aid, service conditions and academic matters.

After completing intermediate studies (Class 12th) conventional courses in science, arts and commerce and vocational courses are offered. Moreover, 29 vocational courses are also offered in 588 junior colleges in the field of engineering and technology, agriculture, home science, paramedical, business and commerce and humanities.

Collegiate Education

The department of collegiate education ensures quality, equity and access to higher education for the students.

Further, it monitors academic quality in 126 government degree colleges and 69 aided colleges existing in the state.

The department also looks after the development needs of all government colleges.

There are 195 degree colleges (126 government and 69 aided) with 1,46,124 students (87,339 in government colleges and 58,785 in aided colleges).

Technical Education

The department of technical education strives to bring out engineers and technicians with adequate skill sets to match the demands of the industry.

At present, there are 1,356 diploma and degree-level professional institutions in Telangana with a total intake of 3.47 lakh students per year.

Skill Development Centres

To improve the quality in technical education, 27 Skill Development Centres (SDC) have been set up in polytechnics at a cost of Rs 30 lakh for each SDC which offered hands-on training to enhance the employability of students. As many as 10,028 students were trained at SDCs till the end of 2014-15.

Higher Education in Telangana

As majority of higher education institutions are located in Hyderabad, Rangareddy and Warangal districts, access to these colleges for earning a job-providing degree is quite difficult for most of the rural students of Telangana.

EDUCATIONAL SYSTEM OF TELANGANA

The regional and official language of Telangana is Telugu. Other linguistic groups in the state include speakers of Urdu and Hindi. Telangana Education is offered through a number of institutes spread across the state. In Telangana the education system is of 10+2 system before joining under graduation. First standard to Tenth standard classes are conducted by the School Education under the administration of the School Education Department and finally the Tenth Class (S.S.C.) Public examination at state level is conducted by the Board of Secondary Education. After this two year Intermediate Education under the administration of the Board of Intermediate Education. The state would provide reservation in higher education to weaker sections of society on the pattern of Tamil Nadu, bypassing the 50% limit.

Schools

Telangana has a number of public and private schools and these are either affiliated to the Board of Secondary Education Telangana (BSE,Telangana) or Central Board of Secondary Education (CBSE), ICSE, IB, IGCSE. Government of Telangana is working towards building the excellent school system.Telangana is the 5th place for education passing percentAge of 2018

Universities

Universities include:

- Dr. B.R. Ambedkar Open University, Hyderabad
- English and Foreign Languages University, Hyderabad
- Jawaharlal Nehru Architecture and Fine Arts University, Hyderabad
- Jawaharlal Nehru Technological University, Hyderabad
- Jogulamba Mahila University, Mahbubnagar
- Kakatiya University, Warangal
- Kaloji Narayana Rao University of Health Sciences, Warangal

- Mahatma Gandhi University, Nalgonda
- Maulana Azad National Urdu University, Hyderabad
- Osmania University, Hyderabad
- Potti Sriramulu Telugu University, Hyderabad
- Rajiv Gandhi University of Knowledge Technologies, Adilabad
- Sri Konda Laxman Telangana State Horticultural University, Hyderabad
- Telangana University, Nizamabad
- University Arts and Science College, Warangal
- Symbiosis International (Deemed) University

Institutes

Institutes include:

- Birla Institute of Technology and Science, Hyderabad
- International Institute of Information Technology, Hyderabad
- National Institute of Fashion Technology, Hyderabad
- Nizam's Institute of Medical Sciences, Hyderabad
- School of Planning and Architecture, Hyderabad

Research Institutes

Research Institutes include:

- CR Rao Advanced Institute of Mathematics, Statistics and Computer Science, Hyderabad
- Electronics Corporation of India Limited, Hyderabad
- National Institute of Animal Biotechnology, Hyderabad
- National Institute of Rural Development, Hyderabad
- Tata Institute of Fundamental Research, Hyderabad
- Tata Institute of Social Sciences, Hyderabad
- Indian National Centre for Ocean Information Services, Hyderabad.

Bibliography

Ardley, Bridget.*India.*Englewood Cliffs, N.J.: Silver Burdett Press, 1989.

Atri, Ajit : *Gandhi's View of Legal Justice*, New Delhi, Deep and Deep Pub., 2007.

Barker, Amanda.*India.*Crystal Lake, Ill.: Ribgy Interactive Library, 1996.

Burman, J.J. Roy: *Gujarat Unknown : Hindu-Muslim Syncretism and Humanistic Forays*, Mittal, Delhi, 2005.

Coleman, James S. and Rosberg jr., Carl G.: *Political Parties and National Integration in Tropical Africa*, Berkely, 1964.

Cumming, David.*India.*New York: Bookwright, 1991.

Das, Prodeepta.*Inside India.*New York: F. Watts, 1990.

Ghoshal, U. N.: A *History of Indian Political Ideas*. London, 1966.

Gupta, L.C., M.C. Gupta, Anil Sinha and Vinod K. Sharma *Gujarat Earthquake 26 January, 2001*, Indian Institute of Public Administration, Delhi, 2002.

Huang, Chi-fu: *Foundations of Financial Economics,* Prentice-Hall, 1988.

Hunt, E. K. *History of Economic Thought, A Critical Perspective,* New York, HarperCollins, 1992.

Jack Kemp: *A Monetary Agenda for the World Economy,* Boston, Quantum, 1984.

Jain S.C. *: New Trends in Rural Marketing*, RBSA Pub, Delhi, 2011.

Jeffrey D. Jones: *Handbook of Business Valuation*, New York: Wiley, 1992.

Judith, E.: *The Sexual Exploitation of Panchayati Raj*, Cambridge, Polity Press, 1986.

Kalman, Bobbie.*India: The Culture.*Toronto: Crabtree Publishing Co., 1990.

Kalman, Bobbie.*India: The Culture.*Toronto: Crabtree Publishing Co., 1990.

Kamble, N. D.: *Deprived Castes and their Struggle for Equality*, Ashish Publishing House, New Delhi, 1983.

Kelly, F. P.: *Charging and Accounting for Bursty Connections*, Massachusetts, MIT Press, 1997.

Kenneth L.: *Ahmedabad: A Study in Indian Urban History*, Berkeley, University of California Press, 1968.

Kieve, L.: *Urban Land Economics*, London, MacMillan Press, 1977.

Loomes, G.: *Current Issues in Microeconomics*, New York: St. Martin's Press, 1989.

Maheshwari, Shriram: *Rural Development in India: A Public Policy Approach*, New Delhi, Sage, 1995.

Marino, Andy: *Narendra Modi: A Political Biography*, HarperCollins, Delhi, 2014.

Martin, Gerald D.: *Determining Economic Damages*, Santa Ana, CA: James Publishing, 1995.

Mathur, Y. B.: *Women's Education in India 1813-1966*, Asia Publishing House, 1973.

Mazumder, Sukhendu : *Politico-Economic Ideas of Mahatma Gandhi : Their Relevance in the Present Day*, New Delhi, Concept Pub., 2004.

Mehta, Nalin and Mona G. Mehta: *Gujarat Beyond Gandhi: Identity, Conflict and Society*, Routledge, Delhi, 2011.

Menon, V. P.: *The Transfer of Power in India*, Bombay, Orient Longman, 1957.

Morris-Jones, W.H.: *The Government and Politics of India*, London, Hutchinson, 1971.

Pandian, Jacob.*The Making of India and Indian Traditions.*Englewood Cliffs, N.J.: Prentice Hall, 1995.

Index

L

M

N

O

P

Q

R

S

T

V

W

❑❑❑

www.ingramcontent.com/pod-product-compliance
Ingram Content Group UK Ltd.
Pitfield, Milton Keynes, MK11 3LW, UK
UKHW042017290726
14061UKWH00001BB/35